KW-051-443

Land, Property and
Construction
in the People's
Republic of
China

Land, Property and Construction
in the People's Republic of China

Anthony Walker

Professor of Surveying
University of Hong Kong

A study sponsored by

Levett & Bailey Chartered Surveyors
Hong Kong

Hong Kong University Press

Published by Hong Kong University Press
University of Hong Kong, Pokfulam Road, Hong Kong

ISBN 962-209-270-5

Printed in Hong Kong by Caritas Printing Training Centre

CONTENTS

ILLUSTRATIONS

TABLES

PREFACE

China's struggle to develop its economy and improve the material well being of its population has been in progress since the end of the Cultural Revolution and has gathered momentum since 1980. Important facets of China's 'modernization' have been the reform of land policies, the improvement of efficiency of the construction industry and the attraction of foreign investment.

These three aspects are closely linked in providing the infrastructure and building assets required by mature and progressive economies. China has a long way to go to, but it is clear that the role of land and construction in this process is fully understood. Translating this understanding into reality, however, requires a level of application that is often difficult to achieve.

The reorientation that has taken place in China's communist state to allow the acceptance of the principles of paying for the right to use land, profit making by construction companies and earning of bonuses by workers, has been dramatic. So has the attraction of foreign investors to joint ventures with Chinese companies. The reform of land and construction policies has allowed these companies to provide the infrastructure and buildings needed for their businesses, which have contributed substantially to improving China's economy.

My observations of these processes made me believe that they should be documented as major landmarks in the redirection of the world's most populous country. The impact on the world's economy, if China succeeds with its modernization programme, will be immense and, should a property market emerge, it will have a dramatic effect on the world's property industry.

This book therefore aims to describe the events that have taken place in the modernization of the land and construction aspects of the economy of China and to record the present stage of development. Two aspects of its treatment of the topic are particularly significant.

Firstly, land and construction are dealt with in the same study. Too frequently they are considered to be separate components of the economy. This is patently unsound. Land, buildings and infrastructure development are inseparable, each depends on the other for economic and social viability. To achieve more rapid development, China still needs to recognize this principle and reflect it in its economic, political and administrative structures; although, encouragingly, it has been recognized in the drafting of some recent regulations.

Secondly, the study deals with the domestic aspects of both land and construction whilst also covering aspects relating to foreign joint ventures. Its orientation is the reform of the land management system and the structure and nature of the indigenous construction industry. Chinese foreign joint ventures are then dealt with within the context of China's domestic land development process, which constitutes the vast majority of activity within this sector.

The joint venture content draws upon my previous book, co-authored with Professor Roger Flanagan of the University of Reading, *China: Building for Joint Ventures,* published by Levett and Bailey. I owe a debt of thanks to Roger and all who assisted in its preparation. I am also extremely grateful to many other colleagues and friends for their help and wise counsel: to K. M. Chau, F. Y. Kan and Francis Lau for their deep understanding of China's reforms; to Adam Chan for the details in his dissertation; to colleagues in the Department of Surveying at the University of Hong Kong, particularly Keith McKinnell, for their observations; to John Ratcliffe, Liu Hongyu and Simon Tsui of Hong Kong Polytechnic for their recent good work on the subject, and their previous colleague Bob Couchman for his contribution; to Professor Wang Xianjin and his colleagues at the State Land Administration and the China Land Society for their insights; to Professor Lu Qian of Tsinghau University for his experience. My grateful thanks are also due to the computing staff of the Department of Surveying for creating the diagrams and particularly to Flora Hui for battling through my many drafts and delivering an immaculately typed manuscript. As always, my gratitude goes to my wife for more patience, tolerance and encouragement than anyone can expect.

Nevertheless, the responsibility for any faults that remain is solely mine; there would simply have been many more without the assistance of those whose help I gratefully acknowledge.

Anthony Walker

LEVETT AND BAILEY

THE SPONSOR

The research on which this book is based has been sponsored by the firm of Levett and Bailey Chartered Surveyors. The firm was established in Hong Kong in 1962 and from a small beginning the practice has grown with the economic expansion of Hong Kong until today it is one of the largest in the Pacific Rim with fourteen partners, nineteen associates and personnel of more than three hundred and fifty in Hong Kong. The firm is experienced in all aspects of property and cost consultancy and the practice provides a wide and comprehensive professional service to its clients, encompassing all the economic and financial implications of property development, ownership and investment.

From its base in Hong Kong, Levett and Bailey has progressively expanded overseas, and has established a network of branch offices and joint partnerships in Singapore, Malaysia, Taiwan, Thailand, Japan, San Francisco and throughout Australia and New Zealand.

The firm is also in joint partnership with Hillier Parker of London which extends the geographical range of its professional services to cover the UK, Europe and the USA, in addition to the Pacific Rim and Australia.

Levett and Bailey has worked in China for many years, dating back to 1979 when the firm was appointed for the first high-rise hotel building in China — the Jinling Hotel, Nanjing. Since that time its surveying activities have been extended to Beijing, Shanghai, Guangzhou and many other centres. Projects include hotels, embassy buildings, university buildings, conference and trade centres, commercial and residential developments.

The author gratefully acknowledges not only their generous sponsorship but also the advice, enthusiasm, time, assistance and access to documentation, freely given by the staff of Levett and Bailey.

Tradition and modernization meet as China's land reforms make progress.

CHAPTER ONE
CHINA IN PERSPECTIVE

INTRODUCTION

China's population is over 20% of the total world population and represents about 33% of the population of all developing countries. It is the world's third largest country in terms of land area, after the USSR and Canada. Although it is classified as a developing country and has a per capita GNP amongst the lowest in the world, China does not subscribe to many other measures that define developing countries. China is an enigma.

It lies roughly within the same latitudes as the United States of America. Two-thirds of its terrain, mainly towards the west, consists of mountains, hills and plateaux. Less than one-sixth of the total land area is suitable for agriculture, although yields are high. There are extensive mineral deposits. Geographic size leads to environmental diversity. In the north, extremes of climate and temperature are such that it is possible to build efficiently only at certain times of the year, and some areas are prone to earthquakes. Typhoons on the subtropical south-east coastal belt can attain a wind speed of over 100 miles an hour, with torrential rains and flooding. Figure 1.1 gives some of the facts and figures about this fascinating country.

China's population density varies enormously, from less than 2 persons per square kilometre in Tibet to nearly 2,000 per square kilometre in Shanghai. Population growth has recently declined under the impact of state control. Figure 1.2 indicates clearly the gravitation of major urban areas toward the eastern seaboard and around major river systems. Figure 1.3 shows the relative increase in urban population. While China remains a primarily agricultural country, the urban population is staggering by western standards. It is also growing under the impact of recent policies that have encouraged a shift of investment, management and technical advancement to the cities.

Land Area	9,561,000 km^2
Population	1096 mn (end of 1988)
Main Cities	Population in mn (end of 1988):
	Shanghai 7.33
	Beijing (Peking) 6.80
	Tianjin 5.62
	Shenyang 4.44
	Wuhan 3.64
	Guangzhou (Canton) 3.49
Climate	Continental, with extremes of temperature; subtropical in the south-east.
Language	Mainly Putonghua based on northern Chinese (the Beijing dialect known as Mandarin); local dialects and languages are extensively used.
Measures	Metric system, also old Chinese measures.
Currency	The currency unit since 1955 has been the yuan, known as Renminbi (people's currency). Renminbi 1 yuan (Rmb¥1) = 10 jiao = 100 fen. Exchange rates in 1990: US$1 = Rmb¥4.71; £1 = Rmb¥7.97.
Time	Zone I (Urumqi) 6 hours ahead of GMT; Zones II, III and IV (Chongqing, Lanzhou, Beijing, Shanghai, Guangzhou, Harbin) 8 hours ahead of GMT.
Fiscal Year	January 1 – December 31
Public Holidays	January 1, Chinese New Year (3 days), May 1, October 1–3

Fig. 1.1   China, facts and figures.

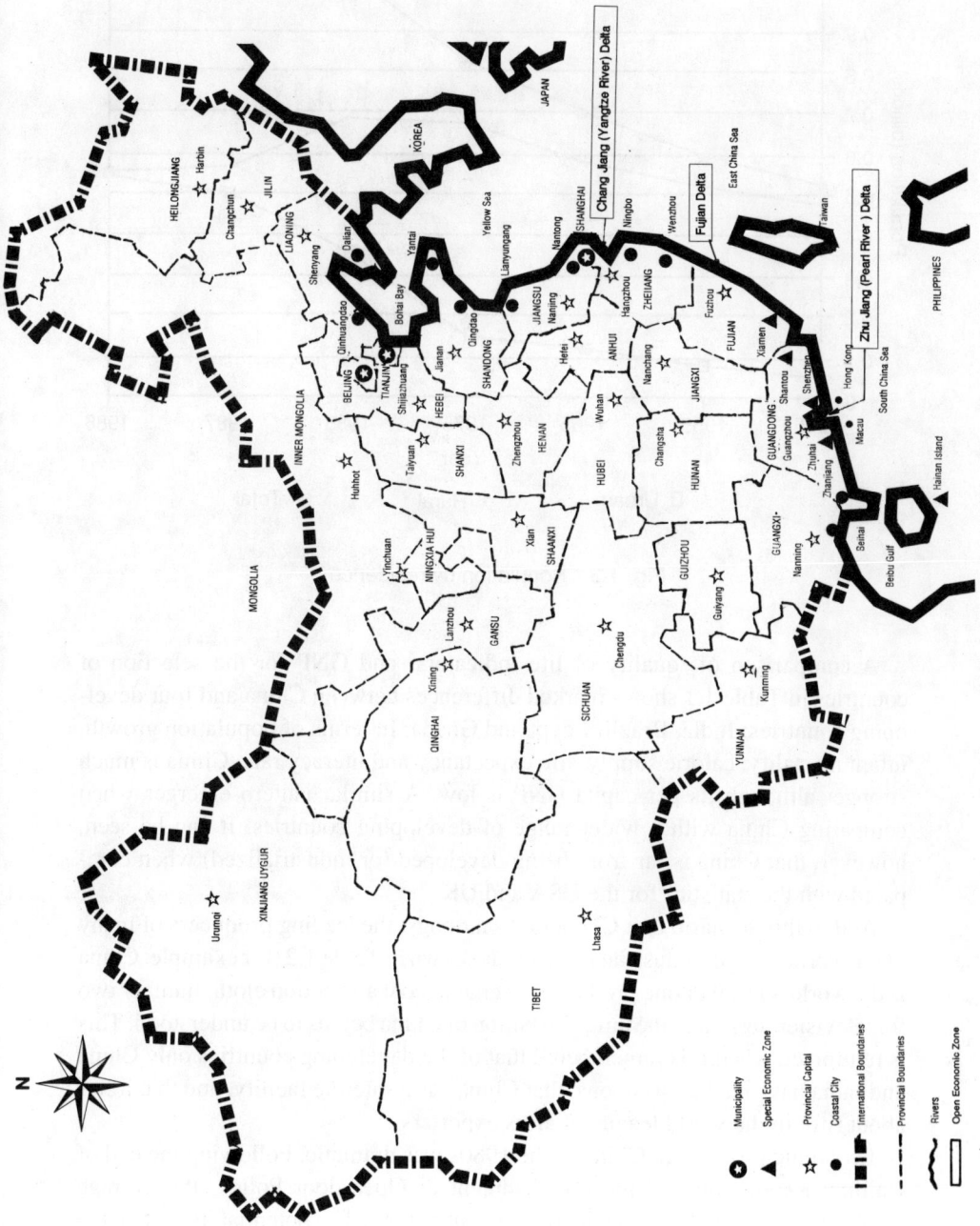

Fig. 1.2 Provinces, cities and investment zones.

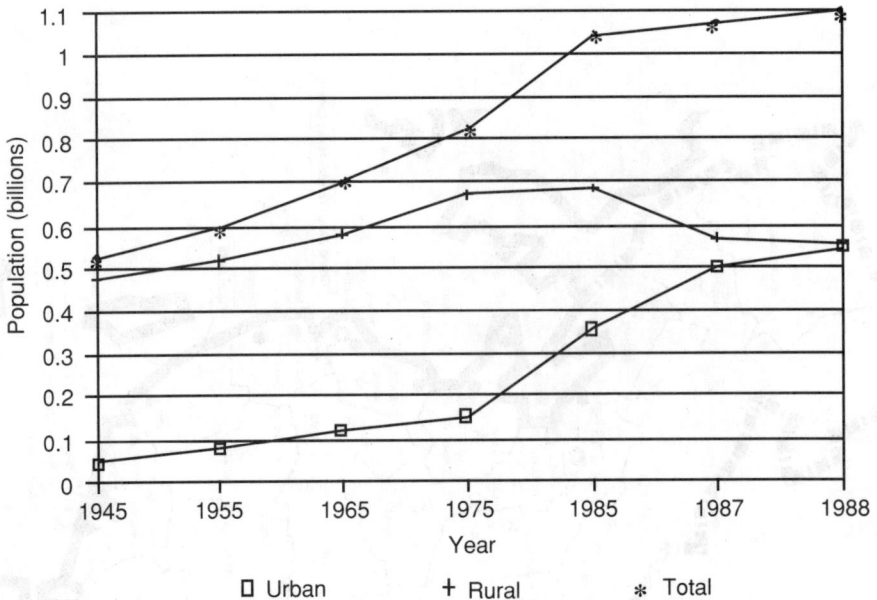

Fig. 1.3 Population by residence.

A comparison of 'quality of life indicators' and GNP for the selection of countries in Table 1.1 shows marked differences between China and four developing countries: India, Brazil, Egypt and Ghana. In terms of population growth, infant mortality, calorie supply, life expectancy and literacy rate, China is much stronger although its per capita GNP is low. A similar pattern emerges when comparing China with a wider range of developing countries. It can be seen, however, that China is far from being developed (or industrialized) when compared with the statistics for the USA and UK.

Add to this scenario that China ranks amongst the leading producers of many of the world's major industrial products as shown in Table 1.2 (for example, China is the world's number one producer of cement, coal and cotton cloth; number two for television sets), and the unique position of China begins to be understood. This is reinforced when it is remembered that of the developing countries only China and India have nuclear weapons, that China has a satellite facility, and that it lies about fifth in the world league of arms exporters.

Economic progress in China in the 1980s was dramatic. Following the end of Cultural Revolution and the establishment of Open-door Policy, the average annual growth rate of national income was about 9%. The potential impact on the world economy of the modernization of one of the world's great civilizations could not have been under-estimated.

Table 1.1
Quality of life indicators.

Country	Population (millions) mid-1986	Population growth rate (%) 1980–86	Infant mortality rate (%) (per 1,000 live births) 1986	Daily per capita calorie supply 1985	Life expectancy (years) 1986	Urban population (%) 1985	Literacy rate (%) 1986	Cultivated land* (%) 1983	per capita GNP (US$) 1986
China	1054	1.2	34	2620	69	22	65	41	300
India	781	2.2	86	2126	57	25	41	60	290
Brazil	138	2.2	65	2657	65	73	75	28	1810
Egypt	50	2.7	88	3275	61	46	38	43	760
Ghana	13	3.5	89	1785	54	32	30	27	390
Malaysia	16.1	2.7	27	2601	69	38	70	13	1830
USA	242	1.0	10	3682	75	74	99	46	17480
UK	57	0.1	9	3148	75	92	99	77	8870

* Includes arable, permanent crop and pasture land.

Table 1.2
China's world ranking as producer of major industrial products.

Product	Ranking (1987)
Steel	4
Coal	1
Crude oil	4*
Electricity	4
Cement	1
Sulphuric acid	3
Chemical fertilizer	3**
Chemical fibre	4
Cotton cloth	1
Sugar	6
Television	2

Source: China Statistical Yearbook 1988
* indicates 1986 figure
** indicates 1985 figure

But overheating of the economy at the end of the decade, the political climate following the events of June 1989, and the reorientation of the once communist states of Eastern Europe have slowed down economic progress and modernization. Chinese leaders continue to say that the modernization programme and the Open-door Policy remain intact, initiatives are still in place and new ones are being introduced.

It should not be forgotten that China is one of the most ancient of human civilizations with a recorded history of thousands of years. Similarly, its history of building reaches back to the Great Wall and beyond. Yet the last decade has witnessed the most significant changes to the previous thirty years of communist rule. Led by the Open-door Policy, these changes have focused attention on China's emergence as a major economic and political power. The powerful political pressures that such economic developments generate, therefore, cannot be under-estimated. That enormous problems have still to be overcome cannot be denied. Their resolution will require one of the greatest national reorientations in the history of the world.

China's approach to land, property and construction has played a fundamental role in its modernization. There are strong signs that this will continue but only time will tell whether a property market will emerge which is capable of maturity and whether economic development can lead to a sophisticated construction industry.

The Open-door Policy

The overriding characteristic of the economic system in the PRC is that it is a communist, state-planned system. Amongst the major changes which have taken place in the last decade are the Open-door Policy and the establishment in the late 1970s of the Special Economic Zones (SEZs) and the Coastal Open Cities, primarily to encourage foreign investment in the PRC. Nevertheless, the PRC is, and can be expected to remain, a centrally planned economy. The suppression of the democracy movements of 1984 and 1989 show the lengths to which the Communist Party has had to go to preserve its control.

In the 1980s, the influence of the Communist Party of China on the day-to-day running of enterprises had been considerably moderated. There had been a general move to investigate and apply capitalist management theory and techniques, and to introduce individual 'responsibility' systems (in western economic terms, incentive-based systems accompanied by the establishment of individual property rights). Both the austerity programme and the political situation held back development of these initiatives but by 1990 they were once again gaining acceptance.

Initially the impact of these changes was most marked in the agricultural sector. Definition of property rights, price flexibility, and the development of a free market for certain agricultural products combined to boost agricultural production and increase peasant incomes. The changes extended to the industrial and construction sectors with, for example, the introduction in 1984 of competitive tendering procedures in the construction industry and the granting of land-use rights by tender and auction to indigenous organizations and, since 1987, to foreign enterprises. By 1988 the economy had begun to overheat and retrenchment was considered necessary. The September 1988 Party Plenum announced that the next two years would be concerned with 'restoring control over the economic environment and rectifying economic order and that price reform in 1989 would be restricted to relatively small steps'.

The economic retrenchment created a situation in mid-1989 in which overheating in the macroeconomy had largely subsided and the accelerating trend of inflation had been halted and reversed. By early 1990 the economy was still deteriorating but the trade situation was improving and China's leaders were becoming rather less preoccupied with the political situation and turning to concern about the economy. They were at great pains to insist frequently that the Open-door Policy remained in place.

Policy Conflicts

State planning and incentive-based competition are not natural partners. Their juxtaposition gives rise to inevitable conflicts and side-effects: evidenced, for example, by overheating of the economy and by charges made by the more conservative elements that change had undermined the socialist development of the PRC. What is being witnessed in the PRC today is an economic experiment of massive dimensions without parallel political reforms. China's isolation has been greatly increased by the political changes in Eastern Europe. Equilibrium, in the system that is being created, is likely to be extremely difficult to achieve.

Following the student demonstrations in 1984, there was a conservative reaction to the students' demands for a more democratic system. Subsequent attacks on liberal thinking showed the conservatism of the Party and evidence of a slowing of political, and to some extent economic, reforms. However, reforms continued but with closer control by government culminating in the student democracy demonstrations of 1989 following the death of Hu Yaobang. The suppression of these demonstrations left China's modernization programme in disarray. Although the Government was quick to state that the Open-door Policy remains intact, many of the industrialized countries on which China depends for economic and technological assistance withdrew their support.

By mid-1990 there appeared to be some relaxation in the hardline approach to both the economy and the political structure of the leadership. Leaders appointed after the Tiananmen incident were making conciliatory statements about both the political and economic situations. It was stressed that economic reform would continue to the extent that an additional Plenum of the Central Committee of the Communist Party was scheduled for mid-1990 to revitalize the economic reforms.

This stance was encouraged by the actions of external agencies. The USA renewed China's Most Favoured Nation status for a further year and the World Bank recommenced some loans. There were also signs of returning investors, particularly from Taiwan. It was reported that the coastal province of Fujian approved 259 Taiwan-funded ventures in the first three months of 1990. There were also political overtures from Taiwan to which China needed to respond.

Nevertheless the outlook is fraught with difficulties in reforming and developing the economy whilst containing potential political unrest. To make solid progress China will need to learn from the Eastern European countries that economic progress cannot take place without political reforms. Against this backcloth China continues to reform its land policies and construction industry.

Many companies still have substantial investments in the PRC which they have to protect. Manufacturing for joint venture companies continues and is likely to do so. For example, between 1.5 and 2 million people in southern China work for Hong Kong companies. Economic activity will not cease, but new investment may be slow, so it will be interesting to observe if internal economic activities and reforms develop in the manner envisaged by the land and construction modernization programme without the stimulus of previous levels of external economic contacts and investments.

Government Administration

The centrally planned nature of the PRC is reflected in its administrative structure. China is governed under a constitution formally adopted in 1982. The highest ranking organ in the hierarchy of state power is the National People's Congress (NPC) with the State Council as the executive organization, both of which are effectively under the control of the Communist Party of China. The State Council administers the country through a series of commissions, ministries, special agencies, offices and administrative units at national level.

Under this structure there are several levels of local government. These consist of three municipalities, twenty-two provinces and five autonomous regions: the geographic extent of these thirty, first order administrative units, is illustrated on Figure 1.2.

The national structure is repeated at each of the lower levels of the administrative hierarchy. This structure maintains central administrative and political control and creates a government bureaucracy which, in common with all bureaucracies, is not conducive to taking initiatives.

Macroeconomic Aspects

Growth

It is only since the mid-1970s that reliable economic data have been made available for the PRC on anything like a regular basis. This renewed emphasis on statistics is a reflection of the changes of the past decade, and of the desire of the PRC to become a member of the international financial community.

China is changing from a predominantly agricultural economy as can be seen from Table 1.3. The shift to a more industrial economy is actually greater than the statistics imply, as one of the idiosyncrasies of Chinese statistics is that rural industrial enterprises are classified under agriculture.

Table 1.4 summarizes the main macroeconomic indicators. Growth has been impressive but dropped to 3.9% in 1989. In 1988/89 the economy had become overheated, and attempts were made, through more closely controlled monetary and interest rate policies, to rein back what threatened to become a headlong rush. Inflation remained persistently high until but was reduced to an estimated 10% for 1990 as shown in Figure 1.4.

At the National People's Congress in 1988, Premier Li Peng said inflation was China's outstanding economic and social problem but that China was still committed to price reform. However, the State Planning Commission confirmed that the prices of 72 major commodities would continue to be tightly controlled and the People's Bank of China began a credit squeeze. Import and export licences and quotas were to be used to regulate trade and the aim was to cut investment in capital construction by Rmb¥50 billion or about 20% of the 1988–89 target.

Table 1.3
Composition of National Income.

Year	Total	Agriculture	%	Industry	%	Construction	%	Transport	%	Commerce	%	per capita
1980	3688	1442	39.1%	1688	45.8%	185	5.0%	126	3.4%	247	6.7%	376
1981	3940	1640	41.6%	1709	43.4%	193	4.9%	130	3.3%	268	6.8%	396
1982	4261	1868	43.8%	1803	42.3%	209	4.9%	150	3.5%	231	5.4%	423
1983	4730	2097	44.3%	1960	41.4%	259	5.5%	160	3.4%	254	5.4%	464
1984	4648	1499	32.3%	2286	49.2%	303	6.5%	203	4.4%	357	7.7%	547
1985	6814	2820	41.4%	2831	41.5%	376	5.5%	236	3.5%	551	8.1%	656
1986	7887	2720	34.5%	3573	45.3%	514	6.5%	308	3.9%	772	9.8%	746
1987	9321	3154	33.8%	4262	45.7%	617	6.6%	349	3.7%	939	10.1%	868
1988	11840	3888	32.8%	5432	45.9%	783	6.6%	438	3.7%	1299	11.0%	1081

(Rmb¥ bn)

Source: China Statistical Yearbook 1989

Table 1.4
Macroeconomic indicators.

	1980	1981	1982	1983	1984	1985	1986	1987	1988
National Income (Rmb¥ bn)	368.80	394.00	426.10	473.00	565.00	703.10	788.70	932.10	1177.00
Index	100.00	106.90	115.50	128.30	153.20	190.65	213.86	252.74	319.14
Exports (US$ bn)	-	22.00	22.30	22.20	26.10	27.30	30.90	39.40	47.50
Imports (US$ bn)	-	22.00	19.30	21.40	27.40	42.20	42.90	43.20	55.30
Retail price index	100.00	102.40	104.40	105.90	108.90	118.50	125.60	134.80	159.70
Exchange rate (Rmb¥ per US$)	1.53	1.75	1.92	1.98	2.80	3.20	3.72	3.72	3.72

Source: China Statistical Yearbook 1989

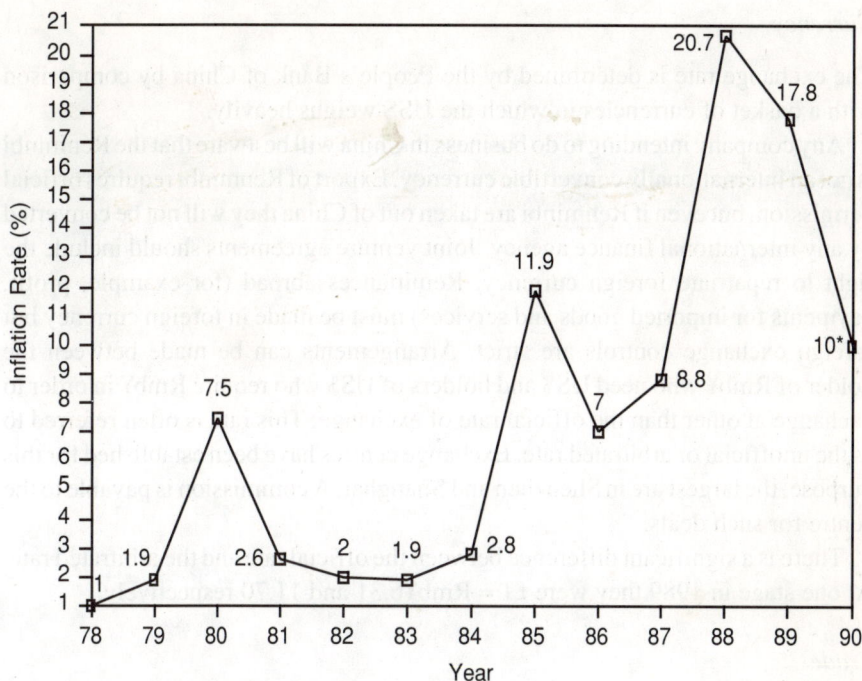

Source: The Economist Intelligence Unit
* estimated

Fig. 1.4 Inflation.

Spending by government departments and other state units grew by an annual average of 21.2% between 1983 and 1988. In the first seven months of 1988 it grew by almost 20% over the previous corresponding period. Chinese foreign trade was increasing substantially in 1988. Exports for the first three quarters were 24% up on the same period in 1987 and imports showed about the same percentage increase.

The tightening of central control and the austerity programme were designed to restrain such growth but also discouraged foreign investors and reduced the availability of foreign currency.

On the road to reform China will continue to wrestle with imbalances in the economic system and with unpredictable political forces. Recognition of the major problem was highlighted by Zhao Ziyang, the then General Secretary of the Communist Party, when he told an international conference in June 1988 that 'price reform is the most difficult problem encountered by all socialist countries in the course of reform . . . we are prepared to take some risks . . . If we can pass this test in five years, China's economy as a whole will be able to shift into an entirely new structure.' Zhao was dismissed from all his posts in 1989 as a result of his support for the democracy movement.

Currency

The exchange rate is determined by the People's Bank of China by comparison with a basket of currencies in which the US$ weighs heavily.

Any company intending to do business in China will be aware that the Renminbi is not an internationally convertible currency. Export of Renminbi requires official permission, but even if Renminbi are taken out of China they will not be converted by any international finance agency. Joint venture agreements should include the right to repatriate foreign currency. Remittances abroad (for example, profit, payments for imported goods and services) must be made in foreign currency but foreign exchange controls are strict. Arrangements can be made between the holder of Rmb¥ who need US$ and holders of US$ who require Rmb¥ in order to exchange at other than the official rate of exchange. This rate is often referred to as the unofficial or arbitrated rate. Exchange centres have been established for this purpose, the largest are in Shenzhen and Shanghai. A commission is payable to the centre for such deals.

There is a significant difference between the official rate and the arbitrated rate. At one stage in 1989 they were £1 = Rmb¥6.31 and 11.70 respectively.

Trade

Traditionally, China has had a relatively low dependence on international trade. The combined value of imports and exports constitute about 18% of national income, slightly more than for the USA. This, however, considerably understates the emphasis placed on external trade as part of the Open-door Policy.

Industrial development is dominated by the desire to produce goods for export, or as import substitutes. The emphasis on heavy industry that characterized the early years of the PRC since 1949 has now been switched to light, technology-intensive industries. There is a growing recognition of the need for quality control, and it was to be expected that the next few years would see Chinese producers making great advances in the range, sophistication and quality of the goods and services they produce.

Japan, Hong Kong, and to a lesser extent, the United States, are China's main trading partners (Table 1.5) with Hong Kong acting as a channel through which access is gained to Far Eastern countries with which China has no formal relations.

Exports consist mainly of raw materials, armaments, foodstuffs and textiles, with oil and coal accounting for a large proportion of raw material exports. Imports, by contrast, consist mainly of finished and semi-finished goods both for consumption and use in manufacturing.

To improve her external trading position, China will need to develop exports of more value-added products and new overseas markets. Recognition of these realities undoubtedly underlay the increased emphasis on the attraction of foreign exchange inflows and inward investment, particularly in joint ventures and

Table 1.5
China's trading partners.

1989	Imports (US$ mn)	Exports (US$ mn)
Hong Kong	24451.2	18865.2
Japan	10844.4	8756.4
Germany	2982.0	2521.2
France	2157.6	1461.6
Italy	1692.0	1276.8
Canada	988.8	945.6
USA	9847.2	5451.6
Australia	795.6	1084.8
USSR*	1802.0	1476.0
UK	882.0	650.4

* 1988

tourism. Constraints on economic growth exist, particularly with respect to shortages of infrastructure, energy and some raw materials and the reaction of investors to the political situation. Congestion of cities, a road system designed for bicycles, horses and carts, and an overloaded rail system were unable to cope with the rapid economic growths. A recurrent theme, in the discussion of difficulties to be overcome in developing the industrial base, is the shortage of energy. Yet China has one of the world's greatest exploitable hydropower resources only 7% of which is currently being tapped.

Similarly, attempts to develop the inland provinces have tended to be less successful, for the perfectly natural reason that these provinces do not enjoy the same advantages of accessibility as the provinces along the eastern seaboard. This disadvantage is exacerbated by underdeveloped infrastructure in many areas.

Urbanization

The urban population of China is large by western standards but this represents a relatively small proportion of total population (Figure 1.3).

A dominant theme in the PRC's recent history has been that communism favours rural development. Marxist theory is essentially pro-rural and the Chinese probably above all others have pursued this socialist ideal. This is a policy whose effects will probably persist and possibly hold back the pace of development of cities and the process of urbanization in China.

In 1949 the urban population accounted for approximately 10.6% of the total population. By 1980 this proportion had increased to around 20% representing an increase over the period of about 0.2% per annum. This low rate of urban growth is quite remarkable and almost unprecedented.

However, one notable feature of China's pro-ruralization period has been the level of industrial growth achieved. It illustrates a very unusual strategy of industrialization without significant urban concentration. In 1980 the index of industrial production (1957 = 100) was 860. This represented an 8.6-fold increase in industrial output in 23 years compared to only a 2-fold increase in the urban population over the same period.

The PRC's urbanization policies had been relaxed coincident with the changes occurring in political and ideological reasoning post-1976. By 1980 an urban development strategy had been formulated, which is designed to 'control the size of large cities, rationally develop medium cities and rigorously develop small cities'. The reality of controlling the size of the larger cities, however, could be a problem. The purpose is to reduce the already substantial urban diseconomies, congestion and environmental problems as well as the potentially high crime rate which has been the experience of many capitalist countries.

In spite of this, the large cities are continuing to grow and production activities have increased in these environments at a faster rate than elsewhere.

FOREIGN INVESTMENT JOINT VENTURES

A cornerstone of the Open-door Policy is the attraction of foreign investment, technology and expertise through joint venture arrangements with foreign parties. Many thousands of overseas firms have been involved in such ventures since 1980. Although they form only a small part of the total economy statistically, they have contributed a disproportionate amount and have given economic and technological impetus to China's modernization programme.

Foreign investment joint ventures in China can take several forms, the most common being equity joint ventures, co-operative ventures (or contractual joint ventures), compensation trade and wholly foreign-owned ventures. The PRC party is usually referred to as 'Party A' and the foreign party as 'Party B'.

Foreign investment joint ventures can operate in a range of economic sectors within the PRC, for example, manufacturing, commerce, tourism. They are all potential clients for the services of foreign and indigenous consultants and contractors as, whatever their area of operation, they are likely to require land, buildings and infrastructure works with which to conduct their operations.

Equity joint ventures are enterprises jointly invested in and managed by a foreign firm, enterprise or other economic organization or individual together with a PRC company, enterprise or other economic organization, which share risks, profits and losses on the basis of equity and mutual benefits.

Equity joint ventures are effectively limited liability corporations, jointly invested in and managed by the foreign and PRC partners.

The share of the foreign partner is generally not less than 25%, and profits are shared according to the equity stake. The equity stake of each partner can take the form of capital or other assets as well as technical knowledge.

Contractual joint ventures or *co-operative ventures,* which are also call 'co-operative management', refer to a contract in which the liabilities, rights and obligations, of the two partners are stipulated through negotiation. Usually under this type of agreement the PRC partners tend to provide land, public utility connections, labour force, or natural resources; whereas the foreign partner may provide capital, advanced technology and key personnel.

Profits, products, risks and liabilities are shared in proportions agreed to in the contract. Upon expiry of the contract, the entire joint venture and its property are turned over unconditionally to the PRC partner of the joint venture.

Compensation trade is a form of direct foreign investment through which PRC enterprises purchase technology and equipment from foreign investors and pay off the principal and interest of the purchase price with products produced with the technology and equipment by instalments or on deferred terms. Management of the production facilities can be expected to be undertaken by the foreign investor.

Wholly foreign-owned ventures are a special kind of equity joint venture in which 100% of the equity is held by the foreign partners. Such ventures form a small but important proportion of foreign investment.

Some indication of the extent of joint ventures is given in Table 1.6. The vast majority of joint ventures are by Hong Kong companies, followed by Japan and the USA but the scale of their investment is much smaller. Hong Kong is by far the dominant external channel for joint ventures, a trend that was steadily increasing.

The largest number of joint ventures are in small scale manufacturing or services, but nevertheless there is a significant number of large value joint ventures. The Chinese authorities have expressed some disappointment that not sufficient investment is in the priority areas such as energy, communications and high technology.

In value terms the municipalities, in particular Beijing and Shanghai, and in numerical terms the SEZs, are the main areas to which joint ventures were directed.

Following the political unrest there was a substantial reduction in new joint ventures. Those in existence continued but problems were experienced by those in process of constructing facilities for joint ventures. The major problem was finance and many joint ventures, both complete and in use and those in the course of construction, had to seek to restructuring of their loans. Most projects eventually continued but at a slower pace. In the case of tourist facilities this could be seen as a benefit as they were not needed until the tourists returned.

By mid-1990, there was activity once again. Much of it was from Asia, particularly from overseas Chinese and of relatively small scale, so that it could be financed internally or with a minor bank loan and did not feature a high degree of risk. It is considered that future large scale joint ventures are more likely to be in

Table 1.6
Extent of joint ventures.

Foreign Investment (January–August 1988)

Type	No. of approved ventures	Contract value (US$ mn)	Actual value utilized (US$ mn)
Equity JVs	2049	1670	695
	(+219%)	(+49.6%)	(+27%)
Contractual JVs	899	846	422
	(+161%)	(+66.5%)	(+8.8%)
Wholly foreign-owned	137	327	231
	(+650%)	(+1260%)	(+558%)
Total	3085	2846	1312
	(+206%)	(+74.6%)	(+25.6%)

Note: Increase over the same period in the previous year is shown in parentheses.

Foreign Investment by Region (1979–87)

	Coastal areas*				Whole nation
	South	Middle	North	Total	
Contract value, share of national total (%)	58.7	12.4	17.5	88.6	US$17.725 bn
Utilized value per capita (US$)	27.09	4.48	5.6	11.74	5.18

Source: Hongkong Bank China Briefing, December 1988
* South = Guangdong, Hainan, Guangxi, Fujian
  Middle = Shanghai, Zhejiang, Jiangsu
  North = Liaoning, Beijing, Tianjin, Hebei, Shandong

the areas of infrastructure, industrial and engineering facilities and buildings in connection with them, rather than hotels and commercial buildings of the immediate past. It is also felt that they are likely to be in the SEZs and open cities of the South where conditions are more relaxed than in the North.

Taiwan has been an increasing source of investment in China, particularly in Xiamen, the Special Economic Zone across the straits between Taiwan and China. Whilst political overtures between these countries remain in an embryo state, China has encouraged investment during 1989/90. For example, it is reported that a Taiwan investor is to build a multibillion dollar naphtha cracking plant near Xiamen for which China have offered a 30 km² site and for which US$7.2 billion has already been pledged.

Officially Taiwan does not allow Taiwanese companies to invest directly in China but many register overseas, particularly in Hong Kong, to undertake investment in China. The unusual nature of the relationship between China and Taiwan is illustrated by the China International Trust and Investment Corporation's (CITIC) intention to open a consultancy office in Taipei aimed at promoting trade between China and Taiwan.

Unofficial Taiwan figures show that more than 300 firms have invested between US$600 million and $1 billion in China. It is felt that Taiwan could follow Hong Kong's example of employing a large workforce in China, particularly in Xiamen.

The Economic Zones

In principle, foreign investment can be undertaken almost anywhere in China. At present, however, the major concentration of this investment is in the Special Economic Zones (SEZs), the Coastal Open Cities and the Open Economic Zones (OEZs), which are located on Figure 1.2. Of course, Beijing, as the capital city, also attracts a large proportion of foreign investment.

The PRC designated the economic zones in order to develop foreign economic relations and trade; in particular, to encourage foreign investment through joint ventures. Special arrangements exist within the economic zones regarding taxation, import levies and such charges, which are designed to provide strong incentives to foreign investors. So far, over 20% of China's total foreign investment has been in these zones.

Fourteen Coastal Open Cities together with five Special Economic Zones (SEZs) in Guangdong and Fujian Provinces and three Open Economic Zones (OEZs) have been designated. These are listed in Table 1.7 and are a strong indication of the serious intention of the PRC to accelerate technical and economic exchanges with foreign countries.

Four SEZs were formally established in 1979, at Shenzhen, Zhuhai, Shantou and Xiamen. In 1984 fourteen coastal cities and Hainan Island were designated as Coastal Open Cities with the power to offer the same incentives as the SEZs. Subsequently, in 1988, Hainan was designated a SEZ. Three OEZs were opened in 1985 in the coastal areas of the Changjiang (Yangtze) River Delta, the Zhujiang (Pearl) River Delta and the southern Fujian River Delta. They were all conceived as export-oriented areas, intended to attract new and advanced technology.

It is primarily through the SEZs, OEZs and Coastal Open Cities that the Chinese hope to secure real technology and knowledge transfer, not only in terms of tangile process and product technologies, but also in terms of knowledge and managerial skills.

The SEZs, OEZs and Coastal Open Cities can be seen as areas of high potential for joint ventures, as through them the Chinese hope to channel a development impulse to the inland provinces and lessen the economic domination of the eastern seaboard.

Table 1.7
Designated areas for foreign investment.

Coastal Open Cities	Special Economic Zones	Open Economic Zones
Beihai	Shantou	Fujian Delta
Dalian	Shenzhen	Yangtze River Delta
Fuzhou	Xiamen	Zhujiang Delta
Guangzhou	Zhuhai	
Lianyungang	Hainan Island	
Nantong		
Ningbo		
Qingdao		
Qinhuangdao		
Shanghai		
Tianjin		
Wenzhou		
Yantai		
Zhanjiang		

The SEZs have led the economic development of China, but the fourteen cities have vigorously competed for investment. In 1986, the government decided to concentrate attention on the best placed cities of Dalian, Tianjin, Shanghai and Guangzhou and give them priority in funding and increased autonomy. About 60% of industrial and enterprises units in the coastal city areas are located in these urban areas and they produce over 75% of industrial value.

The effectiveness of foreign investment policy to attract investment from Hong Kong is shown by almost two-thirds of investment being from that source. It has also been estimated that between 1.5 million and 2.0 million workers in Guangdong Province are employed directly or indirectly by Hong Kong companies. Although they are not all in the economic zones, Shenzhen and Guangzhou have attracted many of them.

The newest of the SEZs, Hainan Island, has more natural resources and is much larger that the older established zones. It is felt that it has the greatest potential for growth in the 1990s. It is more independent than the others, having been subsequently designated as a province and hence only answerable to the Central Government.

Examples of Joint Ventures

Table 1.8 lists some examples of joint ventures projects which are being undertaken in China. This list is illustrative of the range of joint ventures, in terms of business activity, source country and size of investment.

Table 1.8

Examples of joint venture projects.

Announcement date in 1988	Partners	Project	Value	Location	Details
Chemicals					
17 Sept.	China National Technical I/E Corp.; Tecnimont Co., Snamprogetti Co., Italy	Two supply contracts to promote chemical fertilizer industry	US$89.6 million	Sichuan	China will import synthetic ammonia and urea production equipment for the Hejiang Ammonia and Urea Project.
Electronics					
7 Sept.	Elec and Eltek, Hong Kong	Electronics plant project	HK$76 million	Nantou, Shenzhen	Elec and Eltek will lease a 43,000 m² piece of land for 30 years from Shenzhen Nantou Daxin United Enterprise Co. for establishing a new plant which will produce facsimile machines and modems. The output in the first year was expected to be more than HK$100 million.
22 Sept.	Olivetti Hong Kong	A contract to supply and install computer system	HK$9.5 million	Peking & Changshan, Hunan	Olivetti will supply 300 personal computers to 10 secondary schools.
28 Sept.	Olivetti China; Agricultural Bank of China	Supply contract	HK$32 million	Shunde; Wuxi and Wuhan cities	Olivetti will supply hardware and software to the bank and provide training for staff.

Table 1.8 *(Cont'd)*

Announcement date in 1988	Partners	Project	Value	Location	Details
Energy					
19 Sept.	Sunburst Energy Development Inc., a subsidiary of Citic; Jiangsu Investment Corp.; Wuxi Electric Co.; Foster Wheeler Trading Co., Spain; Gruppo Industrie Elettro Mecaniche per Impianti all'Estero, Ansaldo Componenti, Italy	Supply contract to import generators for Ligang Power Plant	US$246 million	Wuxi, Jiangsu	Two 350,000 kW coal-powered units imported from the Spanish and Italian companies.
Property					
22 Sept.	Beijing Municipal Housing Corp.; Groupe Peiege, France	Property joint venture	US$100 million	Peking	A multi-purpose complex, covering 80,000 m², will comprise luxury apartments and studios, offices, shops and amenity facilities.
Textile					
11 Aug.	China United Trading Corp. (CUTC)(50%); Industrial Textile S.A. (INTEX)(50%), Costa Rica	Joint investment	US$3.6 million	San Jose	To export textile products to the third markets. INTEX will provide technology, organization and industrial plants and CUTC will supply raw materials.
10 Oct.	Hangzhou Honglei Silk Weaving Factory; Gunze Sangyo Inc., Japan	Compensation trade agreement	US$ 534,000	Hangzhou, Zhejiang	The Chinese factory will set up a Gunze workshop with 50 weaving machines to establish a kimono silk production base for its Japanese partner. The Japanese will provide all the main equipment.

Transport

Date	Partners	Project	Amount	Location	Description
20 Sept.	Nanjing Motor Vehicle Plant; Fiat Group, Italy	Pick-up trucks project	Rmb¥1 billion	Nanjing, Jiangsu	Aim is to have a production capacity of 1,000 pickups a year by 1990.

Agriculture

Date	Partners	Project	Amount	Location	Description
8 Oct.	Hainan Provincial Agricultural Development Co.; Chia Tai Co., Thailand	Prawn raising joint venture	US$300 million	Haikou, Hainan	To build a prawn-raising centre on about 16,700 ha of beaches. During the project's first phase, they will build a number of 4 ha hatching pools, a 20 ha prawn-raising facility and training centres for personnel as well as a feed plant.

Manufacturing

Date	Partners	Project	Amount	Location	Description
19 Sept.	Shekou Hanshen Co., Jolly Sound; Benelux, Hong Kong	Video cassette plant joint venture	HK$10 million	Shekou, Guangdong	To produce up to HK$35 million worth of video cassettes a year. Benelux will install equipment.
27 Sept.	Shanghai Food Industry Development Centre; Shanghai Investment Trust Co., Coca-Cola Co., US	Shanghai Shen-Mei Beverage and Food Co. (joint venture)	US$18 million	Shanghai	To supply Coca-Cola bottlers with concentrate for making Coca-Cola, Sprite and Fanta. It will also produce the beverage bases for local Chinese soft drinks, make plastic bottles and bottle Fanta and Sprite soft drinks.
11 Oct.	Xian Paper-making Machinery Works; Valmet Paper Machinery Inc., Finland	Xian-Valmet Paper Machinery Inc. (joint venture)	n.a.	Xian, Shaanxi	To increase product variety.
31 Oct.	Hubei Boiler Aided Machine Factory (50%); Diamond Power Specialty Co., US (50%)	Diamond Power-Hubei Machine Co. (30-year joint venture)	US$5 million	Jingshan county, Hubei	To produce high-quality sootblowers and auxiliary apparatus for power plants and the petroleum, chemical, textile, metallurgy and other types of industrial boilers.

Table 1.8 *(Cont'd)*

Announcement date in 1988	Partners	Project	Value	Location	Details
2 Nov.	Zhong Huan Industrial and Commercial Development Co. (40%); Yamaha Corp., Japan (60%)	Musical instruments joint venture	US$16 million	Tianjin	To produce musical instruments.
2 Nov.	Yimin Brewery; Shanghai International Enterprise; Heineken N.V., Netherlands; Chia Tai Group, Thailand	Shanghai Mila Brew Co. (joint venture)	US$30 million	Shanghai	To increase the annual beer production and to renovate the existing facilities, improve technology, train personnel and introduce advanced management.
2 Nov.	Dalian Tape Factory; Dalian International Trust and Investment Co.; Edmin Corp., US	Videotape joint venture	US$7 million	Dalian, Liaoning	To produce 5 million VHS video cassettes annually.
7 Nov.	Beijing Chemical Industry Corp. (49%); Melaka Tong Bee Sdn	United Dragon Corp. (joint venture) Bhd, Malaysia (51%)	US$4 million	Malacca, Malaysia	To begin production late 1989 with an annual output of 12,000 tonnes of rubber compound and 3,000 tonnes of cut thread. 70% of production will be shipped to China.
Others					
16 Aug.	Wong's Kong King (60%); International Trans-Asia Trading Corp.; the franchisee of Brownies in Hong Kong and Macau (40%)	Brownies Food (China) (joint venture)	HK$10 million	Peking	Peking Brownies restaurant will be the first of a whole string of Brownies to be set up in China in accordance with the 35-year agreement which calls for at least 15 stores to be opened in major cities, including Shenzhen, Guangzhou and Shanghai, in the first five years.

Source: China Trade Report

A more detailed example of a large joint venture, which illustrates the significance of financing, is Shajiao 'B' Power Station. However, it should be stressed that this is not typical as there is no one way to structure financing for China projects. Each project represents an individual set of circumstances which requires a tailor-made solution. It should also be pointed out that the climate in 1990 is such that financing such as that described here could be difficult to establish.

In 1984, to alleviate severe shortage of electrical power in Guangdong Province and the Shenzhen Special Economic Zone, the Guangdong Provincial People's Government, in conjunction with the Central Government of the PRC, authorized the development of new power plants at Shajiao. The severe power shortage had been aggravated by rapid industrial developments taking place as a result of the modernization programme and Open-door Policy initiated by the PRC. In 1984, Guangdong General Power Company began construction of the 'A' Station at Shajiao, the first phase comprising 3 x 200 mW coal-fired units.

A little later, the Shenzhen Municipal People's Government established Party A to form a joint venture with Party B to design, construct, commission and operate the 'B' Station which was to be developed on a site immediately adjacent to the 'A' Station. This case study concerns solely the 'B' Station, which consists of 2 x 350 mW coal-fired units designed, constructed and commissioned on a turnkey basis.

Party A is a state enterprise called Shenzhen Special Economic Power Development Company, a vehicle created solely for the purpose of the joint venture. Its role is:

- to provide land and arrange all preferential tax treatment.
- to supply coal to the project at a fixed price and to take and pay for a minimum amount of the designed output capacity of the power plant at a predetermined price throughout the co-operation period;
- to make advances to Party B in certain events where project expenses exceeded project revenue; and
- to pay for electricity monthly half in Renminbi and half in foreign currency. Relative to payment of foreign currency, project expenses including debt service, exchange risks are borne entirely by Party A, in accordance with the terms of the offtake agreement. With regard to remittance of Party B's profit element, the exchange rate risk will be borne 30% by Party A and 70% by Party B.

Party B is a limited liability company called Hopewell Power (China) Ltd., registered in Hong Kong. It is established for the sole purpose of carrying out the project. Share ownership in Party B is as follows:

	Equity (%)
Hopewell China Development Ltd.	50.0
China Development Investment (HK) Ltd.	40.0
Kanematsu-Gosho Ltd.	5.0
Yue Xiu Enterprises Ltd.	2.5
Shum Yip Development Co. Ltd.	2.5

Its role is:

- to be responsible for arranging all foreign currency for financing the project;
- to manage, operate and maintain the project for the ten year co-operation period; and
- to retain 100% of the project revenue during the co-operation period after payment of all project expenses including the cost of coal. At the end of the co-operation period, operation of the joint venture will cease and full ownership and control will be transferred to Party A without any compensation.

The undertakings given by Party A under the coal supply and offtake agreements were guaranteed in terms of performance by Party A by the Guangdong International Trust and Investment Corporation (GITIC). The financing was not entirely guaranteed by GITIC, but the GITIC guarantee can be regarded more in terms of a performance bond supporting the financial obligations of Party A under the offtake and coal supply agreements. In other words, it is like a supply and pay guaranty as well as a take and pay guaranty. Coal will be at fixed price or with financial compensation in the event of failure, and similarly electricity will be paid for whether or not taken as long as the plant is capable of delivery.

A consortium was formed by Mitsui and Company Limited comprising Toshiba Corporation, Ishikawajimi Harima Heavy Industries Company Limited (IHI) and Slipform Engineering Limited (a Hopewell subsidiary) to design, construct and commission the plant on a joint and several turnkey basis in accordance with a contract signed in May 1985. The consortium committed supervisory operating staff during the period of commissioning including completion of reliability trials. Operation of the project was to be undertaken by an experienced and reliable operator appointed for an initial four-year period commencing June 1986 under an operating, maintenance and training contract with Party B.

The total financing requirement was estimated to be about US$520 million. This sum encompasses a fixed construction contract price in respective of civil engineering work, electrical and mechanical equipment. In addition, the estimated cost includes start-up expenses as well as various financing costs including capitalized interest together with insurance costs.

Approximately 90% of the project costs were to be funded by debt financing with the remaining 10% being provided by a combination of shareholders equity, subordinated loans and deferred Renminbi payments under the construction contract.

The debt portion of US$484 million included a Rmb¥ loan of US$ equivalent 92 million, a combination of floating rate HK$ loans and Euroyen loans, with the major source being a fixed rate domestic Yen loan of 49.6 billion or the then US$ equivalent 261 million. The domestic Yen loan took the form of a supplier credit from Mitsui and Company under the export loan programme supported by EXIM

Bank of Japan. This supplier credit was undertaken at a fixed interest rate of 7.3% p.a. EXIM Bank of Japan, however, would not accept the credit risk of the project structure and consequently, the Lead Managers, Citicorp International Ltd., arranged provision of a guarantee facility in favour of the providers of the supplier credit. The guarantee took the form of a letter of credit issued by Bank of China and Daichi Kangyo Bank which banks in turn were secured by counter-indemnities provided by a syndicate of international banks. The same syndicate of international banks provided floating rate Euroyen and Hong Kong Dollar loans. For taking the project risk and indemnifying the supplier credit lenders, the bank syndicate received similar compensation to that provided for in the Euroyen and Hong Kong Dollar facilities.

The critical factors in this project financing were the coal supply and offtake agreements. Coal is supplied at a fixed maximum price and electricity offtake, for a minimum quantity of 60% of production capacity, is also paid for at a fixed price. Electricity is paid for 50% in Renminbi and 50% in foreign currency at fixed exchange rates.

When the original financing package was put in place in April 1986, it included a sum of Yen 49 billion described as the deferred Yen portion of the construction contract price. This was in effect a supplier credit from Mitsui and Company backed by EXIM Bank of Japan. The credit carried a fixed rate of 7.3% per annum with maturity of 1996.

By June 1987, it was observed that Yen interest rate bad fallen and Japanese long term prime rate was approximately 5.5% per annum. Floating rate Euroyen rates were cheaper, however, and it was decided to arrange a refinancing by forming a lending syndicate to provide Yen 49 billion (Euroyen). This was achieved by inviting the syndicate of approximately 50 banks which was then providing a guarantee to EXIM Bank of Japan to change their involvement from that of guarantor to lender.

The banks, therefore, became lenders of floating rate Euroyen and the principal sum was used to prepay the supplier credit. A swap was arranged to convert the floating rate Yen loan into fixed rate Yen and the swap resulted in a favourable fixed rate of interest which enabled the project to save a very substantial sum in terms of interest cost in comparison with the original facility. The projections using the shorter maturity were accepted as realistic following the experience gained from plant operation after the April 1987 commissioning of the first unit.

By then, the shareholders were equally confident that the second unit would be operational by the end of October 1987 which goal was also accomplished. Deemed project completion was to occur at the end of March 1988, therefore, in practice, very early completion was achieved. The period of operation in 1987 saw continuous production well above the minimum offtake requirement of 60% on which cashflow projections were based and therefore the projections can be considered very conservative. The official completion ceremony took place on 29 April 1988 and the Shajiao 'B' Station continues to operate very successfully.

Conflicting Objectives

There are conflicting objectives between the PRC and the foreign investors in joint ventures. Essentially, the Chinese wish to acquire high technology, management and design expertise, and the ability to export high quality goods. They do not want to open their domestic economy to the exploitation that has characterized much foreign investment in Africa, and hope to pay as little as possible for technology and knowledge transfer. The foreign investors, on the other hand, desire access to a potentially massive domestic Chinese market. They are aware of the current problems of using the PRC as an export base. They wish to maintain as much control as possible over their specialist technology and knowledge; if these have to be transferred then the desire is that an economic rent should be paid for the transfer.

It is not surprising that conflicts arise. There is the classic case of two parties to a negotiation, for whom trade will potentially be mutually beneficial, trying to agree upon the distribution of gains from such trade. It is clear that both parties will have to move from their extreme positions: the Chinese will have to grant at least some access to the domestic market and ease the bureaucratic and economic controls on joint ventures, while the foreign investors will have to be willing to accept a degree of technology and knowledge transfer, and to settle for making a normal return on the assets they invest.

THE BANKS AND PROJECT FINANCE

Banks

PRC Banks

Figure 1.5 outlines the many financial institutions within the PRC which are actively involved with development, construction and foreign investment joint venture projects. Many operate under the control of the central bank, the People's Bank of China. It is established as the central bank with supervisory powers over the various specialized banks and financial institutions. It does not handle credit and loan business for enterprises and individuals, but devotes itself to carrying out research and formulating macroeconomic policies, strengthening the management of credits and loans, and maintaining stability of the currency.

Fundamentally two institutions, the Bank of China and the People's Construction Bank of China, are actively involved with financial control. For joint ventures, the Bank of China is the overseas banking arm of the People's Bank of China and operates with the parties involved with the project for matters such as foreign currency and guarantees. Until recently, the People's Construction Bank was only a conduit for distributing state funds for capital projects and dealt with local

```
        ┌─────────────────┐                    ┌─────────────────────┐
        │ People's Bank   │────────────────────│ State Administration │
        │ of China        │                    │ of Exchange Control  │
        └─────────────────┘                    └─────────────────────┘

                  ┌──────────────────────────┐
                  │ Industrial and Commercial │
                  │ Bank of China             │
                  └──────────────────────────┘

                  ┌──────────────────┐         ┌─────────────────┐
                  │ Agricultural     │─────────│ Rural Credit    │
                  │ Bank of China    │         │ Co-operatives   │
                  └──────────────────┘         └─────────────────┘

                  ┌──────────────────┐
                  │ Bank of China    │
                  └──────────────────┘

  ┌───────────────┐   ┌──────────────────────┐
  │ State Council │───│ People's Construction │
  └───────────────┘   │ Bank of China         │
                      └──────────────────────┘

                  ┌──────────────────┐
                  │ People's Insurance │
                  │ Company of China  │            Fund
                  └──────────────────┘            Allocation
                                                  Business

                  ┌──────────────────┐
                  │ Other Financial  │
                  │ Institutions     │
                  └──────────────────┘

                  ┌──────────────────┐          ┌────────────────────┐
                  │ Ministry of Finance │────────│ China Investment Bank │
                  └──────────────────┘          └────────────────────┘

                  ┌────────────────────┐
                  │ China International │
                  │ Trust and Investment │
                  │ Corporation         │
                  └────────────────────┘
```

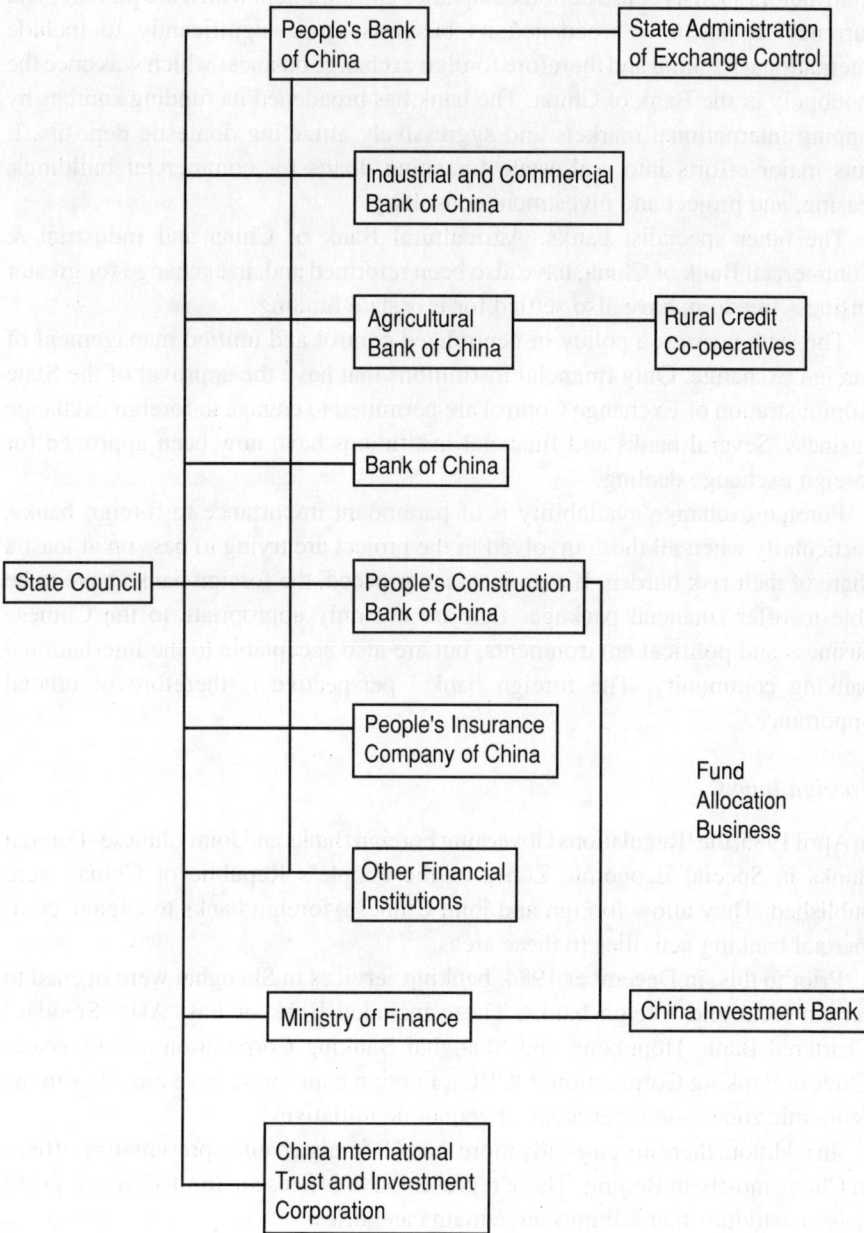

Source: The China Investment Guide, 1986, China International Economic Consultants Inc.

Fig. 1.5   Financial institutions.

contributors such as construction companies and suppliers which are paid in local currency. It has now broadened its business scope significantly to include international banking and therefore foreign exchange business which was once the monopoly of the Bank of China. The bank has broadened its funding sources by tapping international markets and aggressively attracting domestic deposits. It puts major efforts into real-estate financing, loans for commercial buildings, leasing, and project and investment consulting.

The other specialist banks, Agricultural Bank of China and Industrial & Commercial Bank of China, have also been reformed and, in exchange for greater business freedom, have also settled for less state funding.

The state pursues a policy of centralized control and unified management of foreign exchange. Only financial institutions that have the approval of the State Administration of Exchange Control are permitted to engage in foreign exchange business. Several banks and financial institutions have now been approved for foreign exchange dealing.

Foreign exchange availability is of paramount importance to foreign banks, particularly when all those involved in the project are trying to pass on at least a share of their risk burden. If a project is to proceed, the foreign banks have to be able to offer financial packages that are not only appropriate to the Chinese business and political environments, but are also acceptable to the international banking community. The foreign banks' perspective is therefore of crucial importance.

Foreign Banks

In April 1985, the 'Regulations Governing Foreign Banks and Joint Chinese–Foreign Banks in Special Economic Zones of the People's Republic of China' were published. They allow foreign and joint Chinese–foreign banks to engage commercial banking activities in these areas.

Prior to this, in December 1984, banking services in Shanghai were opened to certain local and foreign banks. These included Bank of East Asia, Standard Chartered Bank, Hongkong and Shanghai Banking Corporation and Overseas Chinese Banking Corporation (OCBC). Foreign banks now have branches in the economic zones and other areas of economic initiative.

In addition, there are currently more than 60 foreign bank representative offices in China, mostly in Beijing. These representative offices are limited to non-profit liaison activities that fall into three main categories:

- serving as liaison with Bank of China and other Chinese financial organizations.
- advising and assisting foreign customers doing business in China including arranging financing packages to suit the environment; and
- conducting business development activities with Chinese commercial and trade organizations.

Financing[1]

China has traditionally adopted an attitude of self-reliance when financing development and overseas borrowings have been minimal. Since the early 1980s, the country has remained a conservative borrower but is making greater use of foreign capital and foreign financing, including government assisted facilities and project and trade financing.

China has indicated that its priority for sourcing foreign capital is as follows:

- IMF and World Bank loans and credits;
- government low-interest loans and credits; and
- commercial loans and credits.

China has also forayed into the international capital market in the last few years. In 1987, several PRC institutions issued bonds and certificates of deposit totalling US$2.17 billion.

Mortgage financing is being experimented with in the economic zones. Regulations have been issued and although foreign banks are allowed to advance loans secured by properties, there are still a number of problems to solve before such business become substantial. These include the need for development of legal, registration and foreclosure procedures, and the problem that an enforced sale will generate Renminbi, not foreign currency.

Indigenous Projects

Indigenous construction companies and clients for indigenous projects normally raise finance through loans granted by the People's Construction Bank.

There are two types of loan for investment in fixed assets given by the People's Construction Bank: capital construction loans for new projects and loans for upgrading existing enterprises.

The capital construction loans are only for state-owned companies for their construction projects. The client may apply for loans to the local branch of the People's Construction Bank by submitting completed application form together with approval documents stating that the preliminary design and the preliminary estimates of the project have been approved. The project should have already been included in the government annual plan of capital construction. The annual rate of interest of loan varies for different industries, for example, social purposes attract interest over 50% lower than commercial purposes do.

Loans for upgrading existing enterprises are used for technological renovation or transformation, and for other economic or technical programmes in order to

---

[1] This section draws upon the Hong Kong and Shanghai Bank's Business Profile Series on China and reflects their experience of financing over 400 investment projects in China.

encourage and support companies to develop their production potentiality, to modernize technology and production process and to extend their production output. Such loans are short-term (3–5 years).

The fixed assets loans are made only to state-owned and collective-owned enterprises which are independent economic accounting establishments capable of bearing economic responsibilities and are creditworthy.

In addition, there are reserve loans for capital construction made to client establishments, and advance purchasing and reservation of equipment and materials for projects included in the state plan. They are for equipment listed in the approved design documents that will be delivered to the site but not installed during the planned year.

Also, state-owned and collective-owned enterprises which practise independent economic accounting, hold corporate status, and have opened accounts with the People's Construction Bank are qualified to apply for working loans.

There are many kinds of working loans. They include: working funds loans for construction enterprises, loans for land and real estate development, and loans to enterprises for supplying building materials.

The People's Construction Bank also provides loans to support overseas projects of Chinese construction enterprises. They include revolving funds for projects and loans for export of equipment related to overseas projects.

Foreign Trade and Investment

The financing required for the sale of large items to China and all forms of direct foreign investment in China is, in most cases, in foreign currency. It is therefore important that the parties involved are fully aware of the various options available for putting together a financial package. Local experience and up-to-date knowledge on the most appropriate methods of finance, as well as appropriate forms of co-operation for the ever-changing China market, are most important. Whilst joint ventures may apply to the Bank of China for loans, most joint ventures are financed by external capital in a foreign currency.

Every project in China is unique and therefore has a unique set of financial requirements. The financial package for any given project might use any of the following facilities or a combination thereof:

- term loans;
- government-supported export credit facilities;
- buyer's credit;
- supplier's credit;
- guarantees;
- leasing; and
- capital market instruments.

Potential investors should consider the financial requirements of their proposed project at an early stage of negotiations.

Special Features

Special features of project financing in China are listed below.

- A lender will often want the Bank of China or equivalent guarantees prior to completion.
- Many of the major projects, whilst they may have guarantees regarding the project, also require considerable infrastructure development if they are to proceed on time. Therefore on certain major projects, particularly in the natural resource sector, infrastructure risks can be significant.
- On natural resource projects in particular, there are certain commodity price risks. This is fully reflected in the mineral and petroleum product markets where pay back has been estimated post-construction phase but where commodity price have not increased and, in certain cases, have even decreased.

In the operating phase, foreign banks have previously shown a readiness to lend and to rely on project cash flow for pay back, but even so they are likely to look for certain credit support mechanisms such as:

- sale contracts with reputable parties;
- world prices for the product being used in feasibility calculations;
- protection against inflation and exchange rate fluctuation risks;
- assurance/guarantees to offset any problems regarding commercial contracts particularly with Chinese state entities; and
- a fully committed foreign joint venturer.

A further complication is that whilst bankruptcy laws exist in China, there is a lack of experience, and also perhaps will, in implementing them. In the past bankruptcy was seen as inconsistent with socialist ideology and some of this thinking remains in spite of the law. This is compounded by the lack of a compatible economic environment and real business autonomy leading to enterprises suffering losses due to government policy, not bad management.

The Stock Market

The emergence of securities in the PRC is one of the most significant breakthroughs in terms of both economic and political ideologies. In August 1985, China's first stock market was opened in Shenyang, an important industrial centre in north-east China. Following that, similar markets were opened in Shanghai,

Shenzhen, Wuhan, Guangzhou, Chongqing and Beijing. The shareholding system is now being tried out in over 6,000 enterprises and over 6 billion yuan has been raised. In September 1986 the Guangdong Provincial People's Congress adopted the 'Regulations on Foreign Related Companies in the Special Economic Zones in Guangdong Province' ('The Companies Legislation'). It was the first legislation since 1956 that allows promoters to establish companies limited by shares.

The stock system is more or less a bond market in disguise. In most cases, redemption of the principal is guaranteed by the municipal or county government, e.g., the Foshan issue is guaranteed by the Foshan Municipal Government. In this sense, the issue is without default risk and resembles a bond more than an equity. In more recent issues, however, such as the Guangzhou Commercial City issue, this guarantee was not included. In an announcement made by the Shanghai branch of the People's Bank of China in late 1984, it was stated that shareholders should share the (limited) responsibility of the enterprise in case there was a loss.

Most of the funds raised are used for investing in infrastructure, building, and upgrading of production technologies of enterprises. Funds can be raised for particular projects, e.g., the Nanhai County Government raised funds for the construction of a bridge, which will generate revenue through toll fees. In case of intra-enterprise financing, the enterprise raises funds from its employees to invest in new equipment. In case of forming trust and investment companies, the use of funds is more diversified. The aim of the Foshan Trust and Investment Company is to invest in energy projects, real estate, commercial and industrial projects.

At present the financial market is too rudimentary to provide efficient exchange of existing securities. There is no organized market or well-trained stock dealers. Transfer of outstanding stocks incur extremely high transaction costs although it is allowed. Both the development of enterprises and of financial markets in China are still in their infant stages, therefore it is difficult to establish the price of stocks.

Although provisions contained in the legislation are detailed and familiar to English and Hong Kong lawyers, China has not promulgated a national company law and laws related to securities and the protection of investors. There is no well-established accounting system, or well-trained professionals so there is a shortage of qualified accounting staff.

Also, most of the existing enterprises or companies do not have articles of association, although they do have a board of directors elected by the shareholders.

There are three divergent views on the trial of the shareholding system in China. First, there are those who oppose the shareholding system on political grounds. They believe that it is a prominent feature of the capitalist system through which the working class is exploited, that is, a socialist country's national income should be distributed in a centralized way according to the state plan and that the issue of shares conflicts with state planning.

Second, there are those who consider that the shareholding system should be tried out on an experimental basis by newly established enterprises (mainly collective and co-operative enterprises) with a high risk factor and limited funds, and that buying of shares by enterprises should be promoted but raising of capital by floating shares from the community and individuals should be restricted. Third, there are those who advocate an all-round implementation of the shareholding system. Their main arguments are that a share company is a form by which capital becomes the property of the working classes and that this is a natural progression from the development of a large-scale socialized production and commodity economy.

No more stock exchanges were opened after implementation of the economic austerity programme in 1988. But by mid-1990 reports were appearing which suggested that not only would more be opened but that they would also be more like the stock exchanges in other countries.

Taxation

Domestic Enterprises

One key aspect of China's reform is to give more autonomy to state and collective enterprises so that they become self-supporting entities without having to rely perpetually on state subsidy. It is known as 'li gai shui' or 'replacing profit remittance by taxation'. In principle, an enterprise can now retain the residual profit after paying a flat rate profit rate tax to the state.

Foreign Investors

China has issued numerous laws and regulations on tax matters in recent years but the major ones of interest to foreign investors are:

- the joint ventures income tax law;
- the foreign enterprise income tax law; and
- the individual income tax law.

In addition, there is a value-added tax, the Consolidated Industrial and Commercial Tax, licensing tax on vehicles and ships, customs duties and real estate tax which investors will encounter. There are numerous incentives and exemptions applicable to these taxes depending on the amount of investment and level of technology involved, the length of the project, the economic sector of the project and its location.

Taxes in connection with land and property for both domestic enterprises and foreign investors are considered later.

Hongqiao Economic and Technological Development Zone, Shanghai.

CHAPTER TWO
LAND AND PROPERTY

A PROPERTY MARKET?

Press reports, particularly of the late 1980s, seem to say that a property market exists in China. They speak of land deals, foreign investment, soaring prices and house buying, but the situation needs a closer examination. Some sort of market exists, but in an embryo form. It is unlikely to be a market in a form that is familiar to the capitalist world, but it is likely to be a market nevertheless.

On 1 December 1987, the People's Republic of China auctioned its first piece of land since the communists came to power in 1949. While the auction itself was a remarkable event in a communist state, what was more important was the thinking on land reform policy behind the event. This development was part of the wider modernization which has been taking place since the end of Cultural Revolution in 1976.

Since 1980, thousands of foreign firms have been involved in direct investment in China, and for most joint ventures to be successful they require efficient buildings in which to conduct their operations and accommodate their staff. In putting together joint venture packages the Chinese have invariably contributed land and labour, and the foreigners capital and expertise. In such arrangements, the use value of land becomes important and has become accepted as part of the agreement.

Alongside the Open-door Policy, internal reforms have also taken place. While, as stated earlier, the overriding characteristic of the economic system of the PRC can be expected to remain communist and consequently centrally state planned, there has been a general move to investigate capitalist economic and management theory and techniques, and to introduce to the domestic market incentive-based systems (which translates directly from the Chinese as 'production responsibility systems'). The process has been referred to as 'producing capitalism with Chinese characteristics'. These developments have required a reconsideration of land within the economic framework of a Marxist state, and resulted in the acceptance of the concept that the use of land has a value to the user and that PRC commercial and industrial enterprises can purchase and trade in the right to use land.

China's first auction took place in Shenzhen which borders Hong Kong and is one of the five Special Economic Zones (SEZs) where economic experiments are designated to take place without infringing on the rest of the PRC. Shenzhen is the most developed of the zones, and was chosen as the first one in which land management reforms would be tested. Legislation entitled 'Reform of the Land Management Structure in Shenzhen' was enacted. Documentation to the reform states its aim as being 'to reinforce land-use management, and to exercise state control over existing collective farmlands in the SEZ so that the government can manage and operate the land with a unified policy and management'.

A major purpose according to the reform document is to 'attract foreign investment and to help the development of industries'. The reform also emphasizes three methods — 'negotiation', 'tender' and 'auction' — to allocate land-use rights to various 'institutions' using the land. Political decisions are taken on a site-by-site basis regarding the class of companies which can be the recipients of land-use rights. They may be 'private' or 'public' PRC institutions, foreign companies, or joint ventures depending on the decision in each particular case.

Private real property rights do not exist in the PRC in the same way as in the capitalist countries of the West. All land is owned by the state and originally the reforms use the term land-use rights and not the capitalist terms freehold and leasehold. However, the major legislation on land-use rights in 1990 (Appendix 1) now uses the term lease when referring to the secondary market, but not when the rights are granted by the state — these are still referred to as land-use rights. The establishment of a market in land and property requires a pragmatic view to be taken of Marxism. The PRC has done so by treating property as a commodity subject to the economic laws of commodities for which there is more ideological flexibility and which, they have decided, allows them to sell land-use rights. It all sounds rather contrived, but at least it has allowed the PRC to get off the ideological hook!

Prior to the Open-door Policy and consequent economic reforms, the use value of land was established by the state through central economic planning; as there was no market, the price was purely notional. The use to which land was put and the price charged by the state for use of the land (by state institutions as that is all that existed) was decided by a process of 'negotiation and compromise' between the various ranks of cadres and government officials. The objective was simply to resolve their differences, conflicts and interests and, as a market economy did not exist, the price did not represent value as understood in the West.

After the introduction of the Open-door Policy, the value of the right to use land was recognized, particularly in relation to joint venture enterprises. In addition, state enterprises were required to take responsibility for their own losses and profits. The criteria of competitive performance in deciding rank, bonuses and welfare contributed to keen competition among state enterprises and it has become much more difficult to resolve state enterprises' conflicts and interests merely through 'negotiation and compromise'. As a result, three methods of allocation of land-use rights have been introduced. The PRC has drawn from the experience of Hong Kong in this development as, interestingly, Hong Kong's land is also all owned by the 'state', i.e., the Crown (except for the land on which the Anglican cathedral stands) — a situation which contrasts with its capitalist image.

A major benefit of these developments was the change in procedure so that, rather than applying for a permit for a project and being allocated land only after the permit was obtained, land can now be obtained first without waiting for the project to be included in the annual development plan. The project to be developed is still controlled, but now through the contract for the land-use right which includes planning requirements. This system only applies in areas where land-use reforms are being implemented, e.g., the SEZs. In other areas the traditional allocation system still applies.

At present, the charge of a premium for the use of land through negotiation, tender or auction applies only to a small proportion of land in China. Alongside this system, for the majority of land, is a land-use fee system in which indigenous enterprises are charged for the use of the land they occupy on an annual basis. The system is not yet sophisticated and lacks consistency, but is moving towards a system of economic allocation of land. There are different rates for different uses and locations, and the fee is waived in many circumstances. For example, commercial enterprises may pay full land-use fees, administrative units may pay 50%, land for public housing 20%, schools, parks and temples may be exempt. There may be up to 200% difference between downtown and suburban areas. The fee is usually very low, only a few yuan per square metre per year. A confusion is that often such land-use fees are referred to as annual land and/or property taxes. The latest legislation says that under land-use tax regulations such users have to pay a land-use fee. The terms used, amount levied, exemptions and level of sophistication of the system vary between locations.

When land has been acquired at a premium, an annual land-use fee may or may not be required. If it is, it is often only a nominal sum, equivalent to a ground rent in a UK type system.

The Official View

In April 1988, the 7th National People's Congress passed a most significant amendment to the PRC Constitution which revised Clause 4 of Article 10 from:

> No organization or individual may appropriate, buy, sell or lease or unlawfully transfer land in other ways.

to:

> No organization or individual may appropriate, buy, sell or lease or unlawfully transfer land in other ways. *The right of land use can be transferred in accordance with the law.*

In December 1988, following on from the amendment of Article 10, the 5th Session of the Standing Committee of the 7th National People's Congress subsequently amended the 'Land Administration Law of the People's Republic of China' in a way which further clarified the legality of transferring land-use rights.

It was the first step in reflecting the amendment in the legislation and was at a broadly based philosophical level. It laid down the policies within which subsequent more detailed legislation was to be drafted. The significant provisions were:

- the land-use right of state- or collective-owned land may be transferred through legal procedures. Detailed methods for land-use right transfers will be regulated by the State Council.
- the state practises a paid use land system for state-owned land. Detailed methods of the paid land-use system for state-owned land will be regulated by the State Council.
- prohibition of any occupation of state land or land belonging to a commune, or any sale or letting thereof, except in accordance with the provisions of the law. This clause also empowers the resumption of land belonging to a commune.
- prohibition of the use of land other than in line with the permitted use.
- forfeiture of any monetary gain from any illegal letting or any illegal transfer of land together with fines meted out on the people responsible for such transaction.
- provision that the use of land by joint venture companies or foreign companies will be regulated by other rules to be made by the State Council.

The objectives to be achieved by the provisions were that:

- the state of near anarchy in land use and occupation was to be frozen in its present state before it got even worse;

- any change of use or occupation would have to be approved and registered;
- the power of resumption to the state of any land, not just for implementation of any public works scheme, but also for the need of state-owned enterprises, is reserved.

These amendments have been seen as a landmark heralding the formal establishment of a system of private property rights — a real estate market in China (but it may be a real estate market that is significantly different from any other).

The land tenure system practised in China prior to the reforms, and still existing in most areas today, is that of allocating land to users by administrative means without any charges or limitations on the length of time it could be held.

By virtue of Article 10 of the Constitution of the People's Republic of China, the title to land is vested either in the state in the case of urban land or in the communes in the case of rural or semi-urban land that has not already been vested in the state, and no individual has any claim on the title to any land. Hence the original wording of Article 10 of the Constitution classified leasing as illegal.

According to Marxist theory, land is singled out as incapable of being regarded as a commodity, since it is not a product of man's labour — land exists by itself. Thus, with no one having any title to land and land itself not being accepted as a commodity, it was no surprise that whatever land (or property) market existed prior in China to 1949 quickly disappeared thereafter. The market mechanism was substituted by state allocation of land to the needy, whether it was premises for factories or homes for people. Since no title was given, possession was nine points of the law; since there was no market, registration even of the possessory title appeared to be of no practical purpose and was, therefore, not carried out.[1]

The system was soon shown to be inappropriate to the economic reforms taking place in China because:

- the state derived no direct economic benefit from its land holdings although the occupiers of land were able to turn their possession to economic benefit;
- the lack of a market deprived both central and local governments of the chance of raising finance through land sales for infrastructure development for enhancement of cities and towns;
- it leads to inefficient use of land resources with under and over use of land and lack of flexibility leading to difficulties in relocation;
- the burden of providing housing lay with the state or state-owned enterprises. This leads to immobility of labour which was frequently tied to state enterprises and a lack of responsibility on the part of the occupiers; and

---

[1]   Kan, F. Y. (1989) Reform of Urban Land Management in China. *Hong Kong Surveyor,* Vol. 5, No. 1.

- the system is not conducive to attracting foreign investment into property if land and buildings are held only with an unspecified period of possession and with the occupiers rights not fully and clearly defined.

Professor Wang Xianjin, Director of the PRC State Land Administration and Chairman of the China Land Society, identified that China's reformed land tenure system would have its own characteristics that will produce a market rather different from others. He stated that:

- the reform is not to establish a variety of land ownership forms, e.g., freehold, leasehold. The reform is to commercialize land-use rights, and to apply land rent principles and value laws to the flow of land-use rights.
- the reform is not to weaken state ownership rights of land while strengthening utilization rights of land; instead, it is to strengthen both. The reform is not to change state ownership of land. To enforce state ownership rights is, on the one hand, to fully actualize such right in an economic sense, and, on the other hand, to have an efficient macro- and micro-control of land use.
- the market mechanism is not to be brought to fullest play, but is to be qualified. Not only is there to be no market for free selling and buying of land, but the flow of land-use rights is also not to be completely commercialized. Free allocation of rights shall be continued in certain cases.

The pattern of the reform is to allow the co-existence of two forms of paid land use. One form is collecting annual land taxes, i.e., land-use fees, which, it is said, shall be spread as soon as possible to every city and town and to all factories and mines. The other is to charge a premium (in the words of Wang — 'the form of collecting the total land rent for the entire term of the lease'), which shall be adopted in a few suitable cities.

Such changes have required ideological rationalization and Wang does so by saying that:

> History only finds utopian socialists who claim that the socialist system warrants citizens using public land free of charge. Founders of Marxism foresaw the existence of land rent in a socialist society; even though they thought that that society would be incompatible with a commodity economy.

Engels once said explicitly:

> The end of the private land system does not mean the end of land rent, but it means a shift of land rent — though in a changed form — from individuals to society. That is, working peoples ownership of production means does not rule out the leasing phenomenon. So, to practise paid use of urban land is, among other things, to correctly understand and adhere to Marxist theory of land rent.

It is felt that China has long misused her urban land, not due to state ownership of land, but due to the free use of land without a fixed duration of use, and that Hong Kong's experience is worthy for China to draw upon.

In Hong Kong, all land is owned by government, outlawing free selling and buying of land or private ownership of land; but because it follows the practice of paid lease and transfer of land-use rights, its land market is well developed and has been a mainstay for the region's rapid social and economic progress. For China, with its long established state ownership of urban land, it is felt that the best mode of reform would be a similar one that both promotes forces of production and maintains state ownership of land.

It is felt that the old land-use system actually deprives the state of its proprietary rights of land, but grants land users such rights. Therefore, the reform should not further diminish the state's legal rights but strengthen them by changing the highly monopolized old system. From a macro-point of view, land owner and land user shall form a lessor–lessee relationship; the owner shall claim land rents from the users, thus actualizing its ownership economically. From a micro-point of view, the land owner (the state) can bind land users by setting down such terms as land-use type, duration of house building, conditions for transfer of land-use rights, etc.

The right to use land shall also be strengthened as paid transfer of land-use rights shall be allowed. A lessee's land-use right, since he has paid for such long-term right, is a property right rather than a creditor's right. Before the lease expires, he can legally occupy leased land, gain income from such land, and can also sub-lease or mortgage his right to land use. The reform therefore draws a distinction between commercializing urban land, which is unacceptable, and commercializing the rights to use land, which is acceptable. The policy points out that Hong Kong adopts such a system.

Associated with this point is the need to prevent land profiteering and ensure that land transactions serve the purpose of making proper and economical use of land. Specifically it is stated that:

> Land businessmen make big profits, but society sustains great losses. In our reform, we should be on guard against such losses; we should manipulate land flow into a balanced effect economically, socially and environmentally.

In terms of application and development of the reforms there are two major aspects which should be considered:

- the advantage of a premium payment for land-use rights rather than periodic payments; and
- the need for a series of regulations and standards to be formulated concerning lessee's development of the land from various angles such as urban planning, architecture, transportation, fire fighting, environment protection and affor-estation.

The reform considers that paid transfer of urban land-use rights can only be experimented with gradually in a few cities, such as the Open Coastal Cities and inland cities that are carrying out the programme of comprehensive economic reform.

The problem of the change-over of land tenure systems is recognized by classifying land into 'old land' and 'new land'. 'Old land' is land that has been allocated to the user under the old system for which an annual land-use charge will be levied by the state and a fixed term given. It is expected that this method will eventually disappear as 'old land' acquires a price and is traded. It will be many years before this system can be implemented and it is expected that it will be the next century before use rights for such land are widely traded. 'New land' is land that the state provides. Land users shall pay a premium for the use of such land in the 'pilot cities', e.g., SEZs etc. Annual charges will be made for such land in other areas, presumably in order to control the rate of development. Free allocation of land will continue for government agencies, military and social welfare purposes. The transfer of land-use rights in 'old land' in the pilot cities causes problems due to its rapidly rising value, and methods of taxing gain are being examined. Such transactions in Hainan have resulted in half the profit being turned over to the state.

A further problem is that, naturally, paid transfer of land-use rights ultimately depends on land users' ability to pay them. Some cities have intended to try paid use of land but are afraid that their enterprises cannot afford the charges. Their worries are not groundless. For instance, Shanghai has made several investigations since 1985 into some enterprises' financial capacity, but all have ended with discouraging results. A recent investigation into 714 of Shanghai's industrial enterprises show that even if land-use fees were less than half of what foreign-invested enterprises now have to pay, more than half of them could not carry the financial burden. The land-use charges alone are more than their profits.

A large part of urban land is for residential use. Paid use of land would add to residents' financial burden, which is already heavy enough because of the high rate of inflation. In addition, both the central government and local governments would suffer a financial strain under paid use of land. When municipalities supply 'new land' for capital projects, central government or local governments will have to give financial support, and hence increase the financial burden on them.

It can be seen that China is finding it difficult to set fair standards for land-use charges and for land prices. China would rather have the annual land rent low rather than high. It is considered that too high a land rent would disturb the whole of society and block the way to reform. Yet, a low land rent can be adjusted to a fair one with little inconvenience. One method suggested for setting a premium illustrates China's concern about inflation and escalating land-use prices. It is certainly an unusual approach and is that, prior to auction, a secret price is fixed as the highest to be accepted, when bids reach the secret price the auction stops. If several people offer the same final price, land can be leased to them all as co-developers; if any of them disapproves of co-development, he is seen giving up his right to land use. It is doubtful that such a suggestion has been made before and it is equally doubtful whether it will work, but it is illustrative of official thinking as it tries to grapple with developing a land market in a communist society.

In early 1990, a significant piece of legislation was passed entitled 'Provisional Regulations on the Granting and Transferring of the Land Use Rights over the State-owned Land in Cities and Towns'. This legislation, which is included as Appendix 1, brought together the various regulations used in the cities, economic zones, etc., for the sale of land-use rights, and rationalized and consolidated them for country-wide application.

The regulations include:

- the separation of ownership and the right to use land;
- the right to sell, lease and mortgage land-use rights (LUR);
- registration of LUR;
- details of the contract for the sale of LUR;
- maximum lengths of terms of LUR;
- use of negotiation, tender and auction for selling LUR;
- change of use;
- transfer of LUR (which includes buildings and other structures on the land);
- leasing of LUR, buildings and other structures (but not before development of the land);
- mortgaging LUR;
- termination of LUR;
- allocation of LUR free of premium (usually for social purposes, e.g., schools, hospitals), but subject to a nominal land-use fee;
- proceeds of sale of LUR to be used to develop towns and cities.

In May 1990, rules were published allowing foreign investors to acquire land-use rights, either independently or in joint ventures, for undeveloped land which allowed the foreign investors to provide the infrastructure to enhance the value of the land and bring it into economic production. This significant legislation is entitled 'Provisional Measures for the Administration of Foreign Investors to Develop and Operate Plots of Land' and is included as Appendix 2.

The type of site development referred to includes site clearance, drainage, electricity supply, water services, roads, communication facilities and public buildings.

It also allows for the construction of buildings on the developed land and the leasing of the development.

These rules only apply to the Open Coastal Cities and Economic Zones. They are designed to encourage large tracts of land to be developed such as sections of the Pudong, which has been made available for development in Shanghai.

A further recent piece of legislation which indicates the continuing strong push to land reform is the 'Regulation of Guangdong Province Special Economic Zone for the Administration of Secured Loans'. These are essentially mortgage regulations for situations where the borrower has provided the lender with property as security to ensure repayment of the loan. In the event of a default by the borrower, the lender has the right to foreclose on the property.

An appraisal is required of the property to be used as security for the purpose of determining a value of the property as security. The regulations cover a comprehensive list of requirements to formalize the loan, together with procedures for foreclosure. Requirements regarding maintenance and insurance of the property are also covered.

These three pieces of legislation illustrate the apparent determination of the government to push ahead with land reform.

Negotiation, Tender and Auction

The initial experiments involved disposal by negotiation. In fact this did not differ markedly from the conventional 'negotiation and compromise' method previously used, but nevertheless it was enshrined within the land management reform legislation.

This method is utilized for transactions including:

- government or military institutions;
- public administrations or public utilities; and
- government subsidized institutions for the development of science, education, public health, or sport facilities.

The basic principle is simply to recoup the funds incurred in preparation of the particular piece of land, via a single premium to be paid by the user for the land-use right.

The second experiment involves the sale of land-use rights by tender. The tender documents contain several constraints on the development of the land and require bidders to submit, with their tender, an outline design which complies with the conditions.

The third and most recent of the experiments was to dispose of land by auction. The historic first auction was for a site of 8,588 m^2 with land-use rights for 50 years for residential purposes and took place on 1 December 1987 in the Shenzhen City Hall. For this auction, only PRC state enterprises registered in Shenzhen were allowed to bid and they had to be prequalified. There were 43 registered bidders, of which nine had foreign partners. The successful bidder was the Shenzhen SEZ Real Estate Co., a subsidiary of the Shenzhen Development Co. Its bid was Rmb¥5.25 m (US$1.11 m), which is Rmb¥611 per m^2 (US$130). The company has a monopoly right to sell residential properties in Shenzhen to overseas Chinese.

This gives the company an enormous advantage over its competitors as it will be paid in foreign currency rather than Renminbi, which is not freely convertible. The conditions attached to the sale were:

Permissible gross floor area	15,000 m²
Site coverage	30%
Plot ratio	1.75
Storeys	8 maximum
Set backs	E: 6 m, W: 4 m
	S: 4 m, N: 8 m
Landscape ratio	0.15
Car park	600 m² car parking area to be provided
Development profit	15% maximum
Other conditions	no resale before development or before full payment

The successful bidder stated that his budget per m² gross floor area was Rmb¥350 (US$74) for land and Rmb¥450 (US$95) for construction, giving a total of Rmb¥800 (US$170). With a current selling price of Rmb¥920 (US$195), this would give him a profit of Rmb¥120 (US$25), which is 15%.

The atmosphere at the auction was exciting, and people stood up and clapped to show their appreciation as bids increased; even the auctioneer became excited and was frequently offered advice by the crowd! Each registered bidder was allocated a number, which he displayed on a large card when wishing to bid. At times there were so many displayed that the auctioneer had difficulty in identifying the appropriate bidder.

Shanghai, still the most entrepreneurial city in China, was also one of the first to experiment with land reform. Its first experiment was a tender for land which was opened to foreign investors during the first half of 1988. However, it was won by a state organization, the use of the official Renminbi exchange rate deterring the overseas tenders. Subsequently, many auctions have taken place in areas designated for economic development and are catalogued and discussed later.

Before the reforms, and at present in areas not subject to economic reforms, the PRC charges its state enterprises an annual land-use fee as low as Rmb¥6 per m² (US$1.3) for the use of land. Discounted over 50 years at a rate of interest of around 6%, this is equivalent to a present value of Rmb¥95 per m² (US$20). The prices realized under the reforms show enormous increases.

While these transactions can be seen as transfer payments within the state system and could be dismissed as artificial, it should be recognized that state enterprises are increasingly required to accept responsibility for their profits and losses. As enterprises are increasingly exposed to economic forces, including bankruptcy laws, the value of land will figure in their thinking and be reflected in the embryo market.

However, the above comparison is different if the prices realized through sales to state enterprises are compared with the prices for land use charged to foreign or joint venture companies, which can be strongly influenced by the need or otherwise to attract the investor. This need will be reflected in the negotiation of the land-use charge which results in a very wide range.

The Western press tended to become over-excited at the PRC's adoption of capitalist practices. The Hong Kong press reacted in the same way to the auction and gave the impression that the structure of the PRC's real property rights had undergone a fundamental change leading in the direction of Hong Kong's model for property development. While they may have been guilty of over-reaction, they were right in highlighting a fundamental shift in thinking in the PRC, which may, in the long term, lead to a market in real property.

China is only experimenting — and experimenting cautiously — with capitalist techniques to aid its modernization. This caution is evident in all sectors of the economy including land management. While the privatization of land and property does not depend on how the land-use rights are sold, the tender and auction reforms were a breakthrough in terms of using the criteria of competition among state enterprises and others to allocate land resources.

The austerity programme commenced in late 1988 designed to quieten economic activity and reduce inflation, together with the political unrest in mid-1989, substantially reduced the sale of land-use rights. These events coincided with a decision to end the sale of land-use rights by auction. It was felt that the auction process was adding to price escalation of land-use rights as bidders had frequently not undertaken feasibility studies prior to auction and were bidding far higher than the real land-use value. Public tenders are now used instead of auctions which allow the authorities to eliminate, and therefore not accept, extreme bids.

Private real estate development as conceived in the West is probably inappropriate to the PRC's political structure, and indeed may never be achieved in such a form. At present there are only rudiments of a basic structure of private real property rights and the way in which they will eventually be structured is still unknown. However, the PRC is certainly interested in establishing some type of system of property rights which does not compromise political ideals to too great an extent.

As a result land reform does not seek to totally commercialize land-use rights. For example, land for constructing residential buildings for lower income groups and for public projects will remain to be allocated administratively. A land market in the PRC would therefore be imperfect, i.e., the government, as the owner of urban land, would monopolize land grants through market and non-market means. However, there is the intention to establish a second level market through the transfer of land-use rights between land users as illustrated in Figure 2.1. Second level markets are only emerging in areas where the land reforms have been developing for some time, e.g., the SEZs.

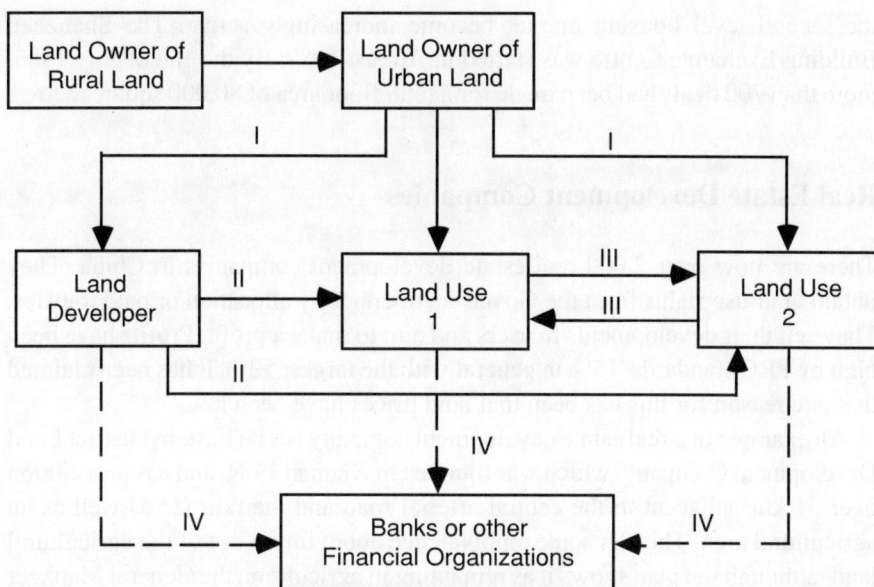

Source: Liu Hongyu, Urban Land Use System Reform in the PRC. Proceedings of the Sympo-
          sium on Construction Project Management in China and Hong Kong, Hong Kong
          Polytechnic, 1990.
Notes: I.   First level market for land-use rights transfer monopolized by state land administra-
                tion authorities.
          II.   Second level market for land development, composed mainly of various kinds of
                real estate development corporations, who invest in development projects in the
                land acquired from the government and then assign the land-use rights together
                with the building and/or structures on the land to assignee.
          III. Third level market for land-use rights assignment between land users, admini-
                stered by the real estate administration authorities.
          IV.   Mortgages of land-use rights.

Fig. 2.1   The structure of the land market.

   Currently, the second level land market is mainly through selling commodity
housing to enterprises or individuals by development companies. For example, in
the Shenzhen SEZ there are now more than 50 real estate development companies.
They are independent economic entities set up to specialize in managing commodity
housing construction, but the scope of their business has already expanded to
construction of factories, warehouses, shopping centres, office buildings, harbour,
highways and other engineering facilities. Between 1980 and 1987, the total
investment on commodity housing was Rmb¥2.28 billion, completed floor area
was 4.45 million square metres, about 31% of total building stock in Shenzhen, and

the second level housing market become increasingly active. The Shenzhen Building Exchange Centre was started in August 1987. By the end of July 1988, more than 700 deals had been made for a total floor area of 80,000 square metres.

Real Estate Development Companies

There are now over 2,000 real estate development companies in China. They obtain land-use rights from the Government either by allocation or paid transfer. They sell their developments to users and aim to make a profit. Profits have been high by PRC standards, 15% in general with the largest 50%. It has been claimed that one reason for this has been that land prices have been low.

An example of a real estate development company is The Eastern District Land Development Company[2] which was founded in Xiamen 1984, and has jurisdiction over 31 km^2 adjacent to the central arterial road and the railroad as well as an agricultural area. There is some ambivalence about future use of the agricultural land; although the plan shows it as remaining in agriculture, the General Manager of the Company said it might be developed after the year 2000.

The Company's Lianhua project, started in 1984, will, when finished, house 25,000 people. By 1988, 4,000 apartments had been built, housing 10,000 people; there also are kindergartens, a primary and a middle school, shops, offices and industrial development. Housing standards are high by PRC standards: 15 m^2/capita, and, for some local and foreign professional workers, 25 m^2/capita.

The site, of which 1 km^2 is destined for residential development and 0.7 km^2 for industrial development, was farmland owned by the state and tilled by 700 farmers.

The Company received the land free from the state, but was required to provide jobs and housing for all of the farmers. Since they were not trained for construction work, this has been difficult. The General Manager suggests that it should be a municipal responsibility to undertake retraining and to provide housing for people displaced by new development.

The Company is responsible for financing its projects. Thus far, 80% of development cost has been raised by sale of apartments and 20% by a loan at 6.6% interest from the People's Construction Bank. Such loan terms average three to five years.

In 1985 and 1986, most of the housing was bought by work units for their employees; these work units include some previously located in Xiamen, some from Fujian Province, and some state agencies with Xiamen offices. In 1987 and 1988, most of the housing was bought by investors from Hong Kong, Taiwan,

---

[2]   Strong, A. L. The use of land policies to strengthen economic development policies in Xiamen. Institute of Public Administration, New York, 1988.

Singapore and the Philippines. As funds have become unavailable from Chinese banks, it has become essential to find foreign investors. The purchasers pay 25% on signing the contract, 60% when the building is finished, and 15% when they receive the keys. Purchasers may resell apartments at any price they can obtain, and a number of investors bought with the intent of reselling.

The Company is authorized by the state to earn a 5% profit on development projects. So far, the Lianhua project has earned the Company a 20% profit. Of this, 55% is paid to the state in tax and the remainder is divided as follows: 40% for re-investment; 30% for workers' benefits, including health; and 30% for bonuses.

THE DEALS

The Early Stages

Prior to the landmark first auction, two lots of land had been sold. Early in September of the same year the Shenzhen Government disposed of a 50 year use right on a piece of land extending to 5300 m^2 to the Chung Hong Company (China Aero-Technology Import and Export Company) for a price of Rmb¥200 per m^2 or Rmb¥1.06 million in total. This was quickly followed in mid-September by a disposal by tender of another set of use rights again for 50 years. This involved a 46,000 m^2 residential site, again in Shenzhen, for a price equivalent to Rmb¥368 per m^2 or Rmb¥17 million in total. On 21 September 1987 the Secretary for the Shanghai Municipal Authority Rui Xingwen put forward a proposal to raise funds for the provision of much needed public works programmes by using the proceeds of selling land-use rights in Shanghai. On 10 November the Shanghai Government confirmed the location and size of the first lot to 'test the transfer of land-use rights with a price'.

This hiatus of activity spilled over into 1988 when in mid-January, Shanghai for the first time began employing a system of issuing land registration documents. The State Council had given approval for Shanghai, Qingzhou in Shandong Province and Huaxian in Guangdong Province to be used as test cases for implementation of such a land registration scheme. Since then the State Land Administration has become committed to establishing a formal land registration system which will eventually encompass the whole of China (a daunting task!), but which at present is a pilot study covering 100 counties.

On 27 January 1988, Hainan Island, the most recently designated economic zone, announced ten special policies aimed at facilitating foreign trade, the seventh of which stated that land-use rights could be transferred for a price, mortgaged or rented out. It would also allow foreign investors, groups of companies, sole proprietors as well as joint venture enterprises to develop parcels of land on a contractual basis for a period of 50 years.

These transactions and others took place before April 1988 when the 7th National People's Congress amended the PRC Constitution to formally recognize the legitimacy of transferable land-use rights.

Since then the sale of land-use rights has taken place increasingly in a number of areas specially designated for economic development as shown in the selection listed in Appendix 3.

Although a variety of terms have been granted in the past, the National Legislation (see Appendix 1) has now laid down the following pattern:

Commercial	—	40 years
Residential	—	70 years
Industrial	—	50 years
Social	—	50 years

The power to grant land-use rights exists with the state, provinces and counties, but no lower in the administrative structure.

A minor landmark occurred following the auction of two lots in Shenzhen in May 1988. It provided the first legal dispute involving land sales in China since commencement of the reforms. A disagreement erupted between the purchaser and the Government as to whether residential components proposed for the development had to be confined to what were subsequently described as 'bachelor flats'. This term was appended to the formal contract that was due to be signed after the auction. The purchaser, which was a state enterprise, refused to pay the purchase price as long as the condition remained and the lot was eventually withdrawn. What is perhaps significant was the reluctance of the Guangdong law courts to involve themselves in the dispute.

A further significant development was the disposal of a 12,800 m² lot for mixed commercial/residential use in Shanghai's Hongqiao district. This represented the first international open tender for land in China. The price paid equated to Rmb¥104 million, but the currency in which it was paid was US Dollars, i.e., US$28 million or US$400/m². The winner was an overseas Japanese–Chinese entrepreneur Mr Paul Sun whose company, Sun's Enterprises, has extensive commitments in Hong Kong. This transaction was a first for a number of reasons:

- it was the first international open tender for land since the reforms;
- it was the first time payment for land had taken place utilizing foreign currency;
- it was the first time an overseas company had won in open competition;
- it was the first time that a valuation for land had been openly carried out by an overseas (Hong Kong) firm of surveyors.

Appendix 3 shows the hiatus in sales of land-use rights as a result of the austerity programme and the political disturbances in mid-1989. It also shows that deals did not really recommence until late 1989 and into 1990, and that they were predominantly with domestic PRC companies. A notable exception was a 5.3 km² tract of land granted at US$3.25 per m² to the USA company, MGM Development Co., in Tianjin in August 1989. The 70-year lease is for land in the Tianjin Economic Technological Development Area. The company plans to develop an industrial park over the next five to seven years to accommodate 400 fully foreign owned export-orientated companies.

By the time the sales in the first quarter of 1990 were taking place, prices had recovered to about the levels of 1988.

Their Locations

The areas of major economic development initiatives have been identified earlier, but it is worth introducing the Pudong which is an area on the eastern side of the Huangpu River in Shanghai. In early 1990, 350 km² of the area was designated as an economic zone for the promotion of investment, particularly foreign investment. It is hoped that it will become a free port and financial centre on a par with Hong Kong.

The Pudong will be able to provide investment incentives similar to these available in Shenzhen and Xiamen. It is estimated that the area's development will cost US$8 billion over 20 years. Foreign companies will be able to acquire 50-year transferable land leases and set up trading companies in the zone.

The first phase is expected to be a deep water port complex at Waigaoquiao in the north-east area of the zone which would act as a free-trade and export processing zone. Later developments planned include an airport and three power stations.

However, there is some scepticism about the prospects for Pudong, in particular whether Shanghai can build the infrastructure quickly and extensively enough to attract foreign investors.

In order to give greater understanding of areas in which development has taken place, a more detailed account of aspects of two rather different types of economic zones in south China are now given:

Shenzhen Special Economic Zone (SSEZ) [3]

Shenzhen Special Economic Zone is the most developed of the SEZs due mainly to its location immediately adjacent to Hong Kong. In the 10 years since 1978, the SEZ has grown to a modern city with a population of about 600,000 from a town

---

[3] Lau, F. (1989) Shenzhen Special Economic Zone, People's Republic of China, Property Review. *Hong Kong Surveyor,* Vol. 5, No. 1.

of only 30,000 people. It has many modern multi-storey buildings including the tallest office building in China with 53 storeys — the Shenzhen International Trade Centre.

About half of the residents are permanent, the other half being transient and brought in from other parts of China to work in the newly industrialized region. The total population is expected to grow to 800,000 by 1991 and the permanent residents to 600,000 and 800,000 by the years 1995 and 2000 respectively.

Shenzhen SEZ ranks highest amongst the SEZs on all counts as shown in Table 2.1. SSEZ rapidly changed from a rigid centrally-planned allocation system for its land resources to a market orientated system. Land use is now allocated through the market mechanism and the prices illustrated in Table 2.2 have been achieved.

Public tender is now the most popular method of disposal although land-use rights are being disposed of by private treaties at market prices. Enterprises which occupy land on the basis of previous state-allocation system are being urged to obtain a formal land-use right for 50 years through the surrender-and-regrant scheme. As the SSEZ continues to expand, increases of 21%, 57% and 76% were achieved in retail sales, light and heavy industrial production respectively between 1986 and 1987.

Table 2.1
Some economic indicators for the SEZs.

		Shenzhen	Zhuhai	Shantou	Xiamen
Area	km²	327.5	15.16	52.6	131
Gross industrial output value					
Light industry	Rmb¥100	66.0	20.2	27.2	34.0
Heavy industry	million	20.2	4.5	11.5	15.3
Total value of retail sales	Rmb¥100 million	43.2	13.8	18.6	18.7
Number of agreements using foreign capital		622	290	314	290
Foreign capital in agreements	US$ million	431	277	136	266
Utilized foreign capital	US$ million	414	202	80	164

(1988)

Source: China Statistical Yearbook 1989

The total area of SSEZ is 327.5 km². Its linear arrangement lends itself to a string of 5 administrative districts all of which are near the Hong Kong border. The area includes 10 industrial districts covering 15 km² and 5 warehouse districts covering 5 km².

The Central Business District is immediately adjoining Hong Kong's Luohu Railway Station on the Hong Kong–Guangzhou line. It is also close to the main vehicular crossing into Hong Kong. All the high-quality office buildings and retail outlets are located here, as are business hotels such as the Century Plaza Hotel and the Asia Hotel. The CBD is fully developed with high-rise buildings, one of which is 44 storeys and another 53.

Demand for high-quality office space has been strong and there have been severe shortages in good locations. The only high-quality office space due on the market soon is the Shenzhen Development Centre providing 160,000 ft². Demand for office space was predicted at 400,000 m² for 1989–91.

Table 2.2
Examples of land-use rights granted in Shenzhen SEZ.

Date	Lot no.	Location	Lease term	Site area (m²)	Plot ratio	Use	Price (Rmb¥ mn)	Accommodation value* (Rmb¥/m²)
25/05/88	H118-2	n.a.	50 yr.	4,691	6.40	C	19.00	633.00
25/05/88	H404-5**	n.a.	50 yr.	9,834	2.25	R	17.20	775.00
28/12/88	H223-1	Luohu	50 yr.	12,214	1.40	R	11.60	678.00
28/12/88	B212-1	Luohu	50 yr.	3,564	2.50	C	8.10	900.00
01/04/89	H404-5	Shangbu	50 yr.	9,571	2.30	R	14.70	699.40
13/05/89	H124-3	Luohu	30 yr.	11,500	1.60	I	9.68	526.00
11/10/89	n.a.	n.a.	n.a.	6,072	2.00	I	0.76	63.00
22/11/89	n.a.	Futian	n.a.	28,063	1.50	I	4.67	111.00
20/06/89	H124-6	n.a.	n.a.	10,000	1.70	I	6.20	364.71
27/06/89	H121-2	n.a.	n.a.	5,207	1.80	I	7.08	755.34
04/90	B206-6	Futian	50 yr.	22,585	1.42	R	33.90	1,057.00
05/90	B206-9	Futian	50 yr.	13,576	1.34	D	8.20	604.00
16/05/90	B206-3	Futian	50 yr.	30,069	1.32	R	48.00	1,212.00
16/05/90	B206-8	Futian	50 yr.	30,544	1.38	R	48.00	1,139.00
16/05/90	B206-11	Futian	50 yr.	21,257	1.43	R	35.00	1,151.00

* Accommodation value is defined as the price of the land-use right divided by the total permitted gross floor area.

** The purchaser defaulted in payment of balance of the purchase price and the lot was withdrawn.

n.a. = not available

R = Residential, D = Dormitory, C = Commercial, I = Industrial

Offices in Shenzhen International Trade Centre in 1989 were:

HK$10–12 p.s.f. unfurnished
HK$15–17 p.s.f. furnished

Residential buildings have been in high demand with 1.2 million square metres needed. Excellent pre-sale results were achieved at record price levels:

Asking price	—	HK$530 p.s.f. high rise
	—	HK$430 p.s.f. low rise
Rentals	—	HK$0.55 p.s.f. high rise
	—	HK$0.45 p.s.f. low rise

Industrial space prices have been controlled by Government at approximately Rmb¥80 p.s.f. for purchase and Rmb¥1 p.s.f. rental, but this policy is changing and market prices will be realized in future. In 1989, there was an estimated demand for 2 million square metres in the next 3 years.

Hotel accommodation had occupancy rates for high-quality hotels running at 85%, with the rate per standard room at about HK$400 per night. Demand is estimated at 6,000 rooms for 1988–91.

Whilst the estimates of demand for space for 1988–91 can now be seen as over-optimistic in the light of events in Beijing, Shenzhen is still one of the most economically active area of the PRC and is considered to demonstrate the success of China's Open-door Policy.

After the political unrest in Beijing in mid-1989, the land administration bureau did not release any new land for about 6 months. By February 1990 there were signs of recovery. Local enterprises were investing again and some foreign investors were returning. Stocks of vacant units were being sold and further improvement was seen in the following month. Prices returned to about those of early 1989. At this time the greatest demand was for residential units with an estimated shortfall of about 20,000.

Guangzhou Economic and Technological Development District (GETDD)

A different style of development area is Guangzhou, one of China's premier cities with a population of nearly 7 million. It is one of the five cities given priority by the State Council for disposing of land-use rights under the land reform measures. It is classified as one of the fourteen Coastal Open Cities encouraged to receive foreign investment.

In 1984, an area of 9.6 km² within Guangzhou was designated as the Guangzhou Economic and Technological Development District (GETDD), and it is planned to grow to 36 km². Its permanent population is planned to be 17,000 and its total population 35,000 in 1990. Ultimately a population of 300,000 is planned for the enlarged area.

GETDD was the first place in China to grant *industrial* land-use rights by tender. (The earlier grants in Shenzhen were for residential use.) This resulted from the issue by Guangzhou Municipal People's Government in March 1988 of 'Procedures for Grant and Transfer upon Consideration of Land Use Rights in Guangzhou Economic and Technological Development District'.

GETDD is run by an administrative committee which represents the People's Government of Guangzhou. It co-ordinates branches of local government, drafts administrative rules, undertakes planning of the zone and enforces regulations. Its major activities are to examine and approve investment projects, to deal with land administration and construction in the District and with taxation. On a broader front, it is responsible for the public services of education, health and culture, and for handling foreign relationships of the District. The Administrative Committee has authority to approve investments not exceeding US$30 million.

By 1990, a significant amount of infrastructure work had been completed, and a power station with a capacity of 19,000 kilowatts had been constructed. By 1989, investment in the District totaled Rmb¥1,647 million of which about 63% had been made by joint ventures with foreign investors or wholly foreign-owned ventures, consisting of 103 foreign investors.

The Administrative Committee have granted land-use rights by tender as shown in Table 2.3. The first two lots were granted in Rmb¥ and the other eight in HK$ to Hong Kong entrepreneurs.

In 1989, the price for residential property was around Rmb¥100 per square foot and for standard industrial buildings around Rmb¥85. The rental level is about Rmb¥8 per square foot per month.

Housing

The progress on the sale of land-use rights, however, is only one part of the picture or symptom of capitalism. At least a year prior to the start of the activity in land-use sales a certain degree of reform was also being experienced in the area of housing. The municipality of Yantai in Shandong Province was the first to attempt to implement reform in this area when rents for residential occupation rose from Rmb¥0.187 per m² to 'rents at cost' of Rmb¥1.28 per m². An affirmation of this nature, i.e., that rents had to be in line with costs, laid the foundation for the 'commoditization' of residential properties.

At the beginning of November 1986 ten residential units in Shanghai were disposed of, after some intense competition, at an average price of Rmb¥520 per m². Sales prices ranged from Rmb¥37,992 for one of the larger units down to Rmb¥15,509 for one of the smaller units.

Other cities followed suit to the extent that the Bureau of Real Estate Management in the Ministry of Construction actually began producing average unit sales

Table 2.3
Examples of land-use rights granted in GETDD.

Date	Lot no.	Lease term	Site area (m²)	Use	Price (Rmb¥ mn)	Accommodation value* (Rmb¥/m²)
27/04/88	GQ-B1-4	50 yr.	15,953	I	4.15	86
08/08/88	GQ-C1-1	50 yr.	15,977	I	4.17	88
19/12/88	GQ-B7-3	50 yr.	10,146	I	2.76	75
19/12/88	GQ-B7-4	50 yr.	8,494	I	2.31	76
19/12/88	SQ-9-(4)	50 yr.	4,348	C/R	3.33	140
06/01/89	GQ-B7-5	50 yr.	8,419	I	2.31	75
06/01/89	SZ-9-(1)	50 yr.	4,333	C/R	3.14	133
16/01/89	SZ-9-(2)	50 yr.	4,054	C/R	3.33	141
21/01/89	SZ-9-(3)	50 yr.	4,105	C/R	3.33	139
28/02/89	GQ-C7-(1)	50 yr.	10,903	I	2.87	75
29/04/89	GQ-B7-2	50 yr.	10,184	I	2.86	78
02/05/89	SZ-8-(2)	50 yr.	4,936	C/R	4.96	182

* Accommodation value is defined as the price of the land-use right divided by the total permitted gross floor area.
C/R = Commercial & Residential Composite, I = Industrial

prices for residential units differentiated by municipal city, medium size city and small cities.

In older city areas, largely due to the higher costs involved in site acquisition, residential prices actually doubled that of newly developed areas. Throughout 1987, there was a continuing trend in residential transactions till in January 1988 the State Council announced that the housing reform commenced in only a few locations in 1986 was no longer an experiment, but was now an integrated part of both central and local government policy regarding housing reform.

Later in January 1988 the first legitimate real estate exchange agency opened its offices at No. 184 Yu Qing Road in Shanghai. This was the first such agency of its type dealing in residential commodity transfers and other private property transactions. It's name was Chu Wei Ou Real Estate Agency. Within five hours of its grand opening it had been involved in over 140 transactions, including both transfers and registrations for acquisition of private real estate.

Then, at the end of January, Shanghai played host to the first Property Exchange Trade Fair in which some 600 units designated as commodity properties totaling some 300,000 m² were listed as being for sale. What was being sold were land-use rights — actual property rights. Negotiation involving foreign currencies mainly by overseas Chinese were also taking place. The highest price paid at the Exchange

Fair was in fact a transaction involving foreign currency where the equated unit price was US$1,000 per m^2. By the second day of the Fair some 252 transactions had been effected involving over 14,000 m^2 of residential space, with over 100 going to private individuals and approximately 130 being sold to state enterprises. Foreign currency deals accounted for less than 10.

On 15 February 1988 the State Council's leading group on housing systems reform announced a scheme of housing reform to be applied to cities and municipalities right across the country. The basic aim of the reform was to alter the method of allocating the housing resources by means of matching numbers required by state enterprises to one using monetary methods. It is an attempt to reform the low rent system of public housing and allow sitting tenants to acquire their residence and take responsibility for it themselves. The aim was that by 1990, with the exception of the more remote and underdeveloped districts, the majority of all cities and towns throughout the country should be charging rents at costs, which should include all the five major cost elements:

- depreciation;
- maintenance;
- management;
- return on investment;
- property taxes.

The aim can now be seen as ambitious in the light of the austerity programme, the political situation and the resulting slow down in economic reform.

Hence, the scale of this market is not yet extensive. Total transactions involve a small fraction of the housing stock. Some people respond by saying that prices are simply too high. But this can only be part of the picture: another reason being the nervousness of individuals to stray too far down this particular route, a view that is reinforced by a 40-year absence of anything resembling a property market, and indeed property as such not capable of being perceived in market terms.

THE ADMINISTRATIVE AND LEGAL STRUCTURE

The highest administrative authority concerning land is the State Land Administration, which was established in 1986 under Article 5 of the 'Land Administration Law of the People's Republic of China'. Its role is to:

- organize central land-use planning;
- prepare policies, laws and regulations and enforce them;
- arrange land registration, statistics and investigations; and
- co-ordinate matters relating to land administration and settle disputes and deal with illegal occupation of land.

The Administration consists of the following departments:

- General Office
- Policy and Regulations
- Land Registration Management
- Land-use Planning
- Prosecutions
- Education
- Foreign Affairs
- Land Surveying

Operating at the state level the Administration is concerned with the broad management of land mainly in the area of policy. Implementation of policy is carried out in the provinces, districts, cities and autonomous regions. Land administration bureaux are established in these divisions to implement policy. By 1989 they were well established at provincial level, but below that level only about 70% were properly established. A confusion is that the provinces, cities, etc., often adopt different names for their local land administration bureaux. The land administration bureaux employed about 70,000 people in 1989 and the number was growing rapidly.

Legislation on land matters follows a similar pattern to the organizations which administer the law. The 'Land Administration Law of the People's Republic of China', which is the highest authority, was made by the State Council and resembles statements of general policy and guidelines. This law requires detailed implementing regulations to be made by the lower levels of regional governments. The lower the level of government, the more detailed the provisions usually are, as they interpret the way in which national provisions will be applied in the local context. In cases of conflict between the two sets of law, those published by the superior law-making organ will prevail.

The State Land Administration recognizes the great significance of a proper legal framework for land-use rights. Whilst the state law is on the statute book much still remains to be done to reflect its spirit at the local level. There is a great variation at this level from the well developed and detailed regulations of Shanghai and Shenzhen to many areas where local regulations do not exist in any form. For example, Shenzhen is governed by the 'Shenzhen Special Economic Zone Land Management Regulations'. Nine subsidiary regulations governing practices in mortgages, registration, land tribunals, etc., have been drafted.[4]

Complementary to the State Land Administration, there exists the China Land Society. The Society is not an official government organ but is essentially a forum

---

[4]   Lau, F. (1989) Shenzhen Special Economic Zone, People's Republic of China, Property Review. *Hong Kong Surveyor,* Vol. 5, No. 1.

for discussion of land matters. Its members include not only staff of the land administration bureaux at various levels but also staff of other government departments that have an interest in land matters. The Society debates all major issues affecting land management before they are encompassed by administrative legislation.

The Society was established in 1980 as a second rank institution and was promoted to a first rank institution in 1986. It has three committees — Intellectual, Education and Publication, and has five groups:

- Land Investigation
- Land Information
- Land Registration
- Land Development
- Land Economics

By 1988, branches of the Society existed in ten provinces with nine others under preparation.

Taxation of Land Transactions

Various taxes apply to land-use right transactions. They vary between locations and can include:

- a grant fee for acquiring the land-use rights;
- ground rent which is paid annually (currently about Rmb¥1 per square metre per year) and may be referred to as a land-use fee or land and/or property tax in some areas;
- contract tax in the case of assignment of land-use rights together with buildings;
- land appreciation tax (this appears to be only in Hainan at present); and
- property tax in respect of land and buildings, which is an annual charge. This tax is also referred to as the Urban Real Estate Tax and is levied on the owner or user of real estate.

Appendices 5 and 6 give examples for Shanghai. In many instances taxes can be reduced or removed completely as incentives, particularly for foreign investors.

Documentation and Conditions

The documents used for tender/auction of land-use rights cover a comprehensive range of conditions associated with the grant of rights. The type of factors they cover can include such matters as:

- land-use right period;
- annual land-use tax;
- development conditions;
- design and construction;
- method of payment;
- signing of the grant contract;
- relationship with municipal services;
- schedule for completion of development;
- assignment and mortgage; and
- maintenance of buildings.

An abridged English version of the tender documents for a site in Guangzhou Economic and Technological Development District is illustrated in Appendix 4. The Chinese version is much more comprehensive, but the English version illustrates the major aspects covered. The English version of the Shanghai Hongqiao documents, part of which is included as Appendix 5, was much more comprehensive.

It can be seen that the development conditions set out tightly the micro planning requirements. They are a condition of the granting of land-use rights and are the mechanism for planning control within the overall plan for the zones. This pattern follows closely that which exists in Hong Kong where detailed planning is controlled through lease conditions.

The overriding legislation that provides the framework for the drafting of sale documents is the 'Regulations for the Transfer of Land Use Rights for Valuable Consideration'. They are drafted for each specific development area and those for Shanghai City are given in Appendix 6.

They cover such matters as:

- ownership (which remains with the state);
- protection of lawful rights;
- terms of grant and extension;
- administrative authority;
- assigning and mortgaging of land-use rights;
- provision of information to prospective grantees;
- privileges for foreign enterprises;
- procedures for direct grant, tender and auction;
- re-possession;
- taxation; and
- settlement of disputes.

In many cases regulations relating to specific areas were drafted prior to the issue of the national regulations on land-use rights in 1990 (Appendix 1). Contradictions can therefore exist between them. Local regulations are much more detailed than the national ones as they are meant for use in implementation, whereas the national regulations are more concerned with policy. An example is that the detailed Shanghai regulations have different lengths for land-use rights for different uses as contrasted to the national regulations. Presumably local regulations will be brought into line with the national ones.

THE PRESENT POSITION

Marx did not completely deny the functions of market for he explicitly allowed market transactions of what he defined as commodities. His whole thesis was largely built on a detailed critique of capitalism and of the relationship between means of production and commodities.

The role of commodities is not denied under communism rather very narrowly defined. What the Chinese authorities are attempting to do as part of their reform policy is to shift the boundaries of definition, such that the right to use and transfer property rights falls under the now much broader heading of commodities (and therefore tradable), and not a means of production. This reform is designed to achieve faster economic growth and gather foreign exchange. This is a vast over-simplification of the intellectual debate that has taken place in China, but illustrative of the issue.

It is critical in trying to assess the scale of change in China to distinguish between behaviour and structure (institutional).

The behaviour of individuals, firms, etc., gives the appearance that the semblance of a market has formed. People to all intents and purposes buy and sell apartments. Firms to all intents and purposes buy land, build factories and operate those factories. They utilize foreign currency and can be repaid in foreign currency. To all intents and purposes the behaviour of individuals, firms, certain government officials and even the language used in defining policy, i.e., 'responsibility contracts' would support the view that a market in real estate is emerging, a system that foreign investors can work within; where capitalists can utilize labour for their own ends (profits).

But the institutional structure has not yet fundamentally changed. For the time being China remains a centrally planned economy with a system based on socialist principles. The Communist Party is still conservative in nature and will for the foreseeable future remain so. As Deng Xiaoping himself has said,

> The existing political system has now proved to be a formidable constraint to furthering the course of economic reform.

The activities seen as the 'market at work' involve only a minute part of the overall stock of land and property in China's vast urban complex and still further is only one small component of a complete market system.

It now appears that the Hong Kong model of land tenure is regarded as suitable for adoption by China because it has the following merits:

- The Hong Kong model, being a leasehold tenure system, allows for absolute perpetual title of land to be vested in the Government as owner of all land. What the people hold is just a leasehold interest. Such a system lends itself to being easily understood in China.
- The Hong Kong model is one that has been well understood and accepted by international investors.
- Because of the resemblance of the two systems, much less effort will be required to move to Hong Kong's system.

The reform of the economy in the PRC must continue for the real estate market to develop. This will require competition between companies, both state and private, without too many state-imposed restrictions and will need consequential changes in attitudes. Whilst great strides have taken place in the last decade, even without the traumatic happenings in June 1989, there were still a number of major obstacles, which resulted from both a lack of political will and administrative inertia. The problems ahead are extremely complex and require reform of the price system and wage structure. Inflation continues to be a severe problem also and the success of the embryo real estate market is dependent upon the solution of such macroeconomic problems within the constraints of political and ideological pressures, which are unprecedented.

Further inhibitions to the market arise from the administrative structure in which property development involves numerous government departments and complex procedures, which confuse PRC companies and which overseas companies or investors could hardly manage to navigate without a state enterprise Chinese partner.

A comparison of land management systems in Guangzhou, Zhuhai and Foshan[5] made a strong recommendation that there should be developed:

- unification of control between urban and rural land;
- clarification of property rights by law;
- unification of the administration of land matters, e.g., policies, laws, planning, administration, registration and management under a land management institution.

In the case of the latter a major current problem is that[6] the functions and relationships between the existing authorities tend to overlap and confusion exists,

---

[5] Liu Hongyu, Urban Land Use System Reform in the PRC. Proceedings of the Symposium on Construction Project Management in China and Hong Kong, Hong Kong Polytechnic, 1990.
[6] Lin Weixin, A comparison of land management systems in Guangzhou, Zhuhai and Foshan. Institute of Public Administration, New York, 1989.

especially in relation to the State Land Administration and the Ministry of Construction (which includes the Real Estate Administration and Urban Planning Administration). For instance, the State Land Administration, through its local bureaux, is responsible for the transfer of land-use rights — representing the government according to Land Administration Law. In some cities, however, the local construction commission also seeks to perform this role because they hold all the registration information relating to buildings and landed property. It is considered urgent, therefore, for the government to clarify the jurisdiction and function of each authority, and to designate a unified, powerful authority to take over the responsibility for land and property administration and construction.

A further major inhibition to a mature market is that Renminbi is not a freely convertible currency, and purchases may be made at the official exchange rate or the 'unofficial' exchange rate between which there is a substantial gap. Similarly the ability to convert income in Renminbi into foreign currency and its transfer overseas may be limited in many cases. Such constraints affect the market in real property, particularly for foreign investors. The achievement of a fully developed international market will only be possible with a more long-term development of the economy as a whole and with the consequential ability to ease restrictions on convertibility of Renminbi and provide access to foreign currencies. Alternatively, if a market restricted only to PRC investors is required, it is likely to take much longer to develop and be less dynamic in the short to medium term.

While land auctions have been high profile events in China, the important issue is how far the PRC will go in legally defining land-use rights as private and enforceable, including not only the right to use but also to transfer, to receive foreign currencies, to lease and sublease. While some progress has obviously been made in relation to allocation of land through a market mechanism, it is only a small but exciting beginning. Only time will tell if this will lead to a substantial market in real property encompassing both state and private developers.

Modern equipment and traditional materials combine
in China's construction industry.

CHAPTER THREE
CONSTRUCTION

Construction in China today is going through enormous changes to make the industry more effective and efficient. Since 1980 the PRC has been intent on moving from an industry rooted in the early part of the century to one typical of the later part.

The construction industry has ambitious targets to meet by the year 2000. The need to improve urban housing, for example, will mean that 3.3 billion square metres of new housing must be constructed, at an average rate of 200 million square metres per annum, about double of the present rate. By any international standards, the size of China's development plans is breathtaking.

In order to meet the new demands, the PRC recognizes that it must change many of its approaches. The Chinese construction industry has, for many years, been plagued with such problems as long construction cycles and poor quality. It is calling for a reform of the industry focusing on less construction time, improved quality, increased returns on investment and introduction of a public tendering system. China is improving its management techniques and adapting to new approaches.

Figures 3.1 and 3.2 put the 1987 construction statistics for China into perspective in comparison with those of a selection of other countries. International comparisons are inherently difficult, but the figures do give an indication of the range of differences. The construction industry in China employs a huge number of people compared to other countries, though this figure is a relatively small proportion of the total labour force (about 4%) by international standards. It

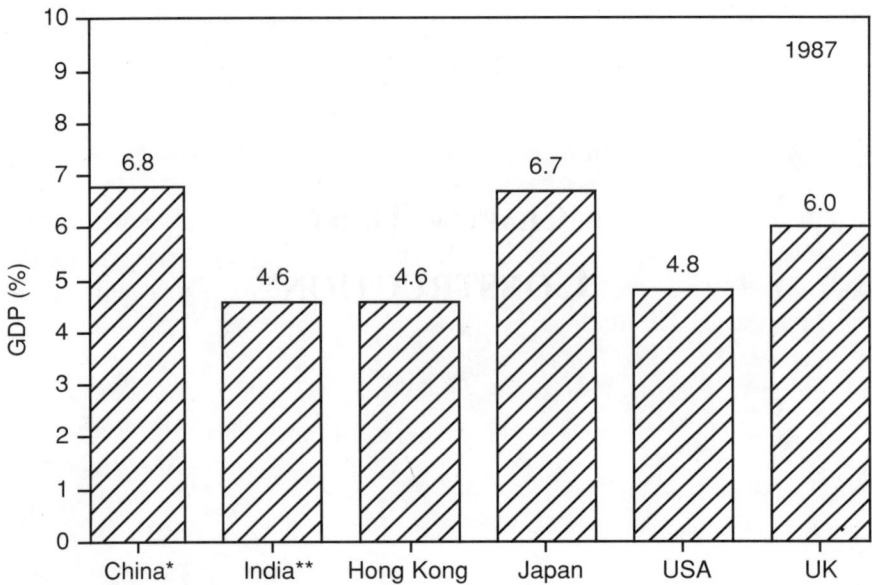

* Approximation based on National Income.
** 1986

Fig. 3.1 Construction output as % of GDP.

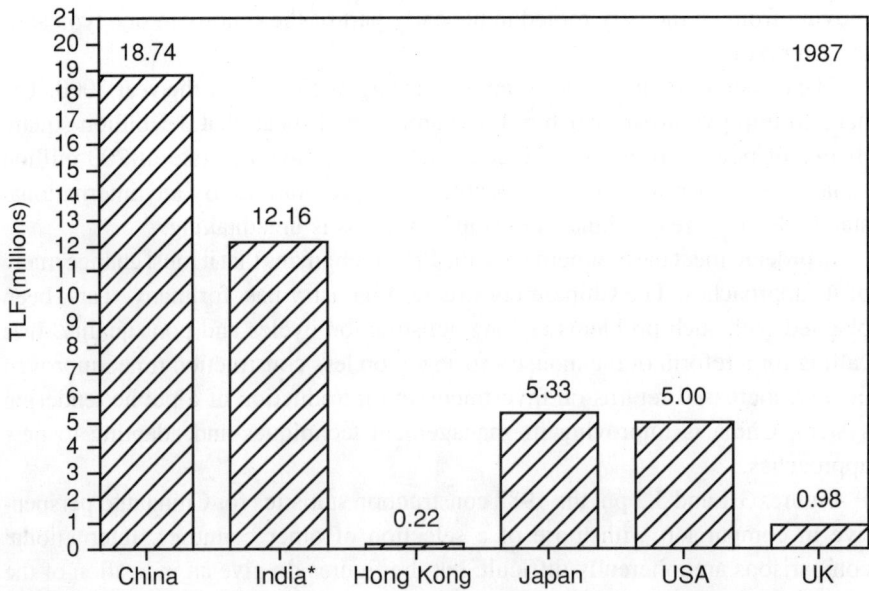

* 1985

Fig. 3.2 Total labour force in the construction industry.

produces a significant proportion of national output, comparable with other economies, and reflects the surge in development in the 1980s.

The changes of the past decade have had three significant impacts on the construction market.

First, the freedom given to enterprises to make investment decisions and to raise funds has led to an increased proportion of construction work being financed outside the state budget, for example, by domestic loans and self-raised finance. The resulting increase in demand for construction work has produced shortages of building materials and generated higher prices. To counter this trend and to contribute to the austerity programme, restrictions on funds were introduced in 1988 and access to loans was limited.

Second, foreign investment as a result of foreign investment joint ventures has been increasing. It is still a relatively small proportion of the total, but represents a large market in absolute terms.

Third, many major construction projects in many regions can now be bid by competitive tenders among construction companies. To a western contractor, competitive tendering may not be a major step, but Chinese contractors have been used to projects being allocated to them.

INDIGENOUS PROJECTS

China's indigenous construction industry has a long history of substantial infrastructure development and of erecting impressive buildings and other structures. In China's rural regions, traditional buildings are of clay, brick, timber, or bamboo; in urban areas, they are mainly of masonry walls, reinforced concrete floor and roof slabs.

Since the seventies, more than 500 high-rise buildings have been built in major cities as apartment houses, hotels and office buildings, with diversified structural systems such as large-size panels, frame, frame-shear wall, shear wall, frame-tube, tube-in-tube. More than twenty of them soar up to 90 m and above, for instance, the 50-storey Shenzhen International Trade Centre is 158.65 m in height. Many multi-story warehouses and stores to take heavy loads and with large interior spaces have been built since 1975, for which the frame or frame-shear wall systems have been adopted. They have been constructed by using table formwork or, more often, by the lift-slab technique.[1]

For public buildings such as sports centres, public halls, theatres, airports, hangars, etc., space grid structures, shells, suspension structures and trusses are

[1]   Lu Qian, Procedure and Practice of Building Design in China. Proceedings of the Symposium on Construction Project Management in China and Hong Kong, Hong Kong Polytechnic, 1990.

often used. Their spans are often 60 m and have exceeded 100 m. The Capital Sports Hall erected in 1968 was designed with an orthogonal space grid structure 112 m long and 99 m wide. The recently completed Shanghai Hall has a grid structure roof of an elongated hexagonal form measuring 60 m x 93.5 m.

Suspension structures have long been in use. The Beijing Workers' Sports Hall completed in 1959 employed a double-layer circular suspension roof structure, 94 m in diameter. The People's Sports Hall in Hangzhou, Zhejiang Province, has a saddle-shaped hyperbolic paraboloid suspension structure roof, measuring 80 m x 60 m.

Three principal organizations are involved in the construction of indigenous buildings in the PRC. They are, using PRC terminology, the development units, the construction units and the design institutes.

The terminology is worth defining:

- a sponsoring client/owner is often referred to as a development unit or sometimes (confusingly) as a construction unit;
- a construction company (sometimes called an operating unit) can be similar to a Western general contractor;
- for indigenous PRC projects, a development unit can build the project by hiring labour and purchasing materials direct, thus acting as a direct labour organization;
- a specialist trade contractor is also called a construction company, but it undertakes only one specialist trade such as piling, painting and decorating, mechanical and electrical services installation (often called engineering installation companies), or lift installation. A specialist trade contractor contracts directly with a construction company in the same way as a Western sub-contractor contracts with a main contractor. Specialist trade contracting is not yet highly developed;
- a design institute is a state or collective owned multi-disciplinary design practice operating mainly within the local government structure.

At all levels of local government, construction is controlled by the local construction commissions or bureaux. Whilst answerable to the local authorities, they are also the administrative arms of the Ministry of Construction. They have under their control the design institutes, construction corporations and companies, building research organizations and all similar entitles concerned with construction.

Design and construction are clearly separated in the PRC. Design institutes are concerned solely with design and construction companies solely with construction. There is no overlap, but recently there has been suggestions that this approach is too rigid and that ways of involving construction companies in design should be found. This is no more than a suggestion at the present time.

A development unit is responsible for initiating a project, obtaining approvals, appointing the design institute and the construction unit and project managing the design and construction processes.

The development unit will prepare a feasibility report, which will include the first estimate of construction cost. This would normally be calculated on a cost per square metre basis. The report is used to obtain approval from the local planning commission and to secure a loan from the People's Construction Bank.

Once the project has been approved the development unit will form a 'preparatory office' to implement design and construction of the project, which in western terms would be an 'in-house' project management group.

The preparatory office will submit the conceptual design documents prepared by the design institute to the local construction commission for approval. These would include an estimate, again normally calculated on a cost per square metre basis.

The same procedure would be carried out with the preliminary design documents and finally with the detailed design documents.

Detailed estimates are priced at rates in Standard Schedules of Rates and Charges. Guidelines for preparing such price books are issued centrally, but each region and municipality has its own version of the book. Differences in prices reflect regional differences in the costs of materials and labour. Prices are updated regularly. Table 3.1 shows an example from a brickwork section.

Traditionally, contractors used Standard Schedule of Rates and Charges to arrive at a price and to negotiate a contract price with development units. Now, contracts are more frequently awarded by competitive tenders and the Standard Schedules used mainly for budgetary purposes, but competitive tenders are still substantially in the minority. Contractors may seek to modify designs to suit their plant and equipment. The amounts of interim payments for work in progress, the valuation of variations and the settlement of the final account will be agreed between contractors and preparatory offices.

Design Institutes

A design institute is a design practice with the professional skills required to undertake a design service, namely:

- architectural design;
- structural engineering design;
- civil engineering design;
- site investigation (including carrying out the actual work on site);
- mechanical and electrical services design (not yet well developed as a discipline);

Table 3.1
An example of the Standard Schedule of Rates.

Item no.	Code no.	Item description	Unit	Unit rate per m³ Rmb¥ 1	Fixed quantity ##	Labour man-day 2	Labour cost Rmb¥ 3	Plant cost Rmb¥ 4	Red brick 1000 brick 5	Cement 325# tonne 6	Lime tonne 7	Sand m³ 8
		3 Brickwork Conveyor belt Transportation										
179	3-3-0	25# brick, above one brick thick internal wall	m³	37.64	10m³	14.32	30.36	11.79	5.21	0.357	0.226	2.53
181	3-3-1	50# brick, above one brick thick internal wall	m³	41.32	10m³	14.32	30.36	11.79	5.21	0.558	0.174	2.53
183	3-5-0	25# brick, one brick thick internal wall	m³	37.75	10m³	14.52	30.78	11.89	5.28	0.341	0.216	2.417
185	3-5-1	50# brick, one brick thick internal wall	m³	41.02	10m³	14.52	30.78	11.89	5.28	0.533	0.166	2.417

Note: The table does not contain all the data necessary for calculating the unit rate. The material contents are given, but the prices of materials are published in a standard material price book.

\# This is a number assigned to classify the standard of the product.

\#\# All costs and quantities of labour, plant and materials are expressed in this unit.

- landscape design;
- cost estimates; and
- interior design.

There is wide variation in the size, scope and abilities of design institutes. The greater part of their workload is for indigenous projects. According to the 'Standards of Qualification-grouping of Design Institutes for Building and Civil Engineering Works' promulgated in 1986, design institutes are divided into integrated or specialized institutes. Integrated ones cover all aspects of design including structural, mechanical and electrical engineering. Specialized units only undertake one or more aspects.

In most design institutes, joint venture design works form a very small but prestigious part of their total workload. Joint venture projects enable design institutes to become involved with high-quality projects, operate alongside foreign designers, and most importantly afford design institutes significant knowledge transfer.

Design institutes lie within the hierarchy of committees established to initiate and control development and construction within each municipality, province and economic zone in which they are located. For example, there are 40 design institutes in Shanghai. The two largest are the Shanghai Municipal Institute of Civil Architectural Design and the East China Design Institute. Each has approximately 900 professional and technical staff and employs a total staff of about 1,400. The smallest has about 100 employees.

The organization structure of which they are part varies between local government regions. In the Shanghai Municipality they are under the Municipal Construction Commission as shown in Figure 3.3. Some large design institutes are responsible directly to the state or partly to the state and partly to the local government. There are also design units, which are collectively owned by the workers, but these tend to operate mainly in the rural areas.

The PRC is not used to package deals or design-and-build approaches where the contractor is responsible for design. The design institutes hold the monopoly on design work, and specialist trade contractors in China do not have the design expertise normally expected of Western trade contractors, although there have been suggestions that they should have.

The design institutes adopt similar practices to foreign designers. They use standard design details for parts of the building and are using computer-aided design packages to produce working drawings.

The scope and expertise of design institutes vary considerably. They are classified in four classes from A to D according to the type, size and location of the work they are allowed to undertake. The highest category of institutes is Class A, registered by the state to work throughout the PRC on projects of any size and complexity.

Shanghai Building Construction Corporation (Bureau) (includes 10 construction companies)

Bureau of Shanghai Municipal Engineering (includes a design institute and about 5 construction companies)

Shanghai Residential Architectural Development Corporation (client body/ development unit)

Shanghai Municipal Construction Commission consists of:
Construction Department
General Office
Scientific and Technological Department
Material and Equipment Department
Building Control Department
Co-ordination Department

Shanghai Residential Building Construction Corporation (includes a design institute and 6 construction companies)

Shanghai Site Investigation Institute

Shanghai Research Institute of Building Sciences

Shanghai Research Institute of Construction Technology

Shanghai Municipal Institute of Civil Architectural Design

East China Design Institute

Over 35 other design institutes (different status although at the same hierarchical level)

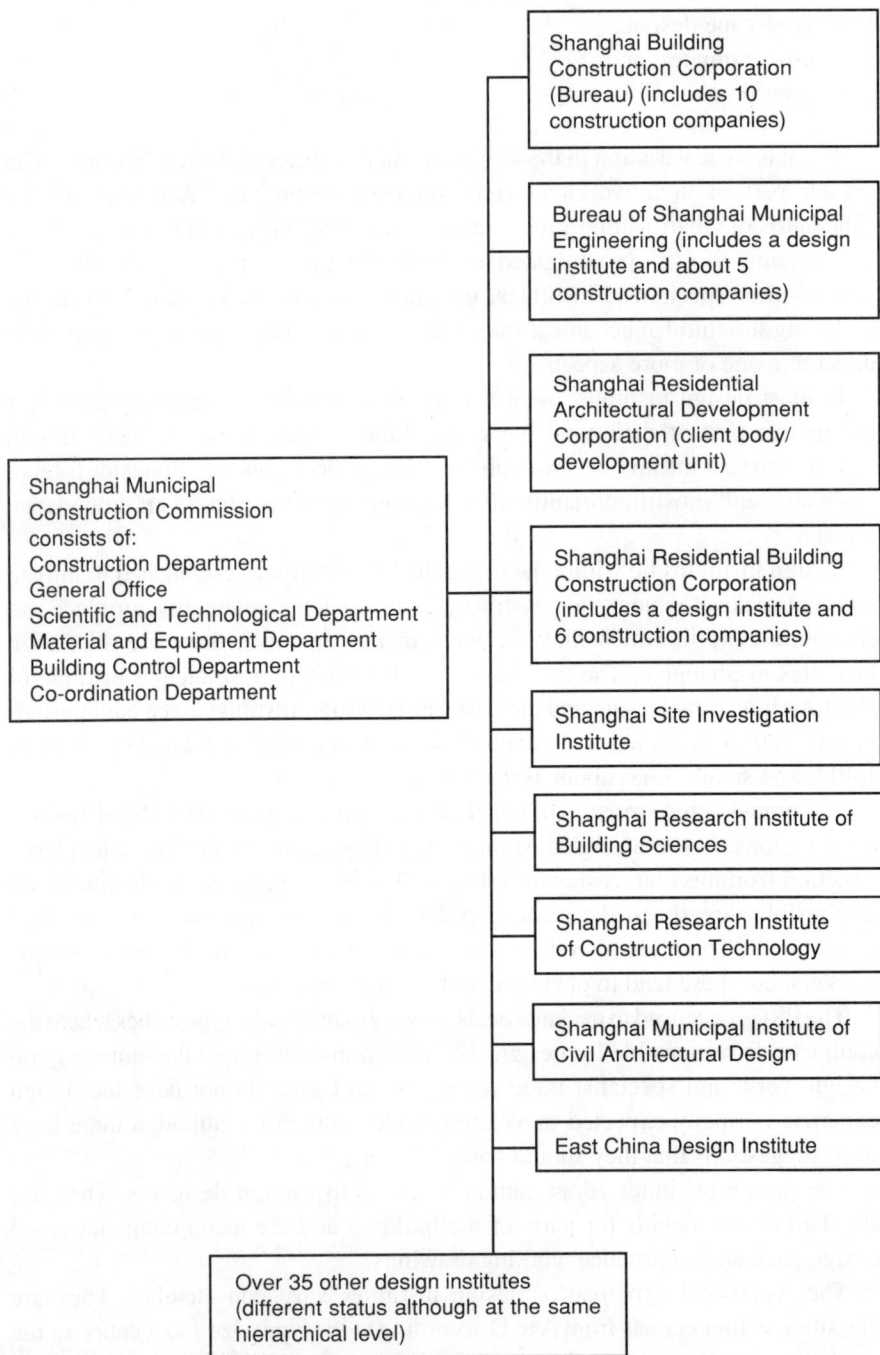

Fig. 3.3 The Shanghai municipality design and construction hierarchy.

Class B institutes can work in local government regions other than that in which they are located, whilst Classes C and D are local design institutes and include the large number of very small collective institutes. The classification of design institutes by number of employees and their qualification is given in Table 3.2 and the types of project on which they can be employed are given in Table 3.3. They may also be approved for building or civil engineering works or both. It can be seen from Figure 3.3 that there is a specialist municipal engineering design institute for Shanghai.

The strength of design institutes lies in structural design. Their staff are academically competent, but, at present, generally lack practical experience in technologically advanced construction, and in architectural design that involves the use of imported materials and technology such as curtain walling, sophisticated mechanical and electrical services, and high-quality finishes.

Stages of the design process and other aspects described later under the Joint Venture section apply equally to indigenous projects.

Preparatory Offices

Traditionally, a preparatory office is established to handle local projects and is responsible for the procedures and submissions for approval, transportation, liaison with fire services, utilities and similar agencies, procurement, post-contract payments and final accounts, and to co-ordinate contractors and materials supply. This office acts as the client's representative to ensure that the project progresses.

It is mainly involved during the construction stage, but its work does overlap the design stage in so far as procurement of construction is concerned. It is staffed by specialists who are responsible for ensuring that all the tasks that are commonly seen to be project management are carried out. The specialists, e.g., engineers, are often permanent employees of the client's organization.

There is a great need to co-ordinate construction companies because, traditionally in China, construction companies have been concerned with supplying labour for specific sections of work, but have not developed strong management skills. Generally, one contractor would build the substructure and superstructure, another the finishes, another the plumbing and so on, with no one contractor being responsible for overall organization in the way a general contractor would normally be in many other countries.

Construction Companies

Some of the PRC's construction companies act as general or main contractors but most act as specialist trade contractors.

Table 3.2

Qualified employees required for different categories of design institute.

Qualification requirements	Group A	Group B	Group C	Group D
1. Backbone designers				
a. Number of persons:				
Architects	5 and more	3 and more	2 and more	2 and more
Structural Engineers	5 and more			
Other specialized designers	3 and more			
b. Education (in their own specialty)	Universities and colleges	Universities and colleges	Universities, colleges and technical secondary schools	Technical secondary schools or higher
c. Practical experience as leading designers	At least for 5 projects of class Extra or class I	At least for 5 projects of class II or higher	At least for 5 projects of class III or higher	At least for 5 projects of class IV or higher
2. Ratio of backbone designers to medium and lower qualified technical personnel	1 to 6	1 to 6	-	-
3. Percentage of designers having university-college education and practical design experience for more than five years from the total number of technical staff	nearly 50%	nearly 40%		
4. Distribution of technical staff among design trades	Comparatively reasonable	Comparatively reasonable	Comparatively reasonable	Comparatively reasonable
5. Management systems for quality and technical control	Comparatively perfect	Good	Fairly good	Necessary
6. Equipment and installations	Sophisticated and complete	Comparatively complete	Fairly complete	-

Table 3.3

The projects that different categories of design institute are allowed to design.

Group of design insitutes		Types and size of projects
A		Projects of any type and any size to be located in any place in the country.
B	1.	High-rise public buildings with height not exceeding 50 m and with fire-proofing grade 2.
	2.	Residential buildings with number of stories not exceeding 18.
	3.	Single-storey public buildings with spans not exceeding 30 m.
	4.	Single-storey industrial buildings and warehouses with spans not exceeding 30 m and crane capacity not exceeding 30 tons.
	5.	Multi-storey industrial buildings and warehouses with spans not exceeding 12 m and not exceeding 6 storeys.
	6.	Structures such as chimneys, water towers and tanks.
C	1.	Multi-storey public buildings with height not exceeding 24 m.
	2.	Single-storey public buildings with spans not exceeding 24 m.
	3.	Single-storey industrial buildings with spans not exceeding 24 m and crane capacity not exceeding 10 tons.
	4.	Multi-storey industrial buildings with spans not exceeding 9 m and not exceeding 4 storeys.
	5.	Medium-sized and small chimneys, water towers and tanks.
D	1.	Houses, dormitories and other public buildings with brick walls and reinforced concrete floor slabs and not exceeding 6 storeys.
	2.	Public framed buildings with spans not exceeding 7.5 m and not exceeding 3 storeys.
	3.	Single-storey public buildings with spans not exceeding 15 m.
	4.	Single-storey industrial buildings and warehouses with spans not exceeding 15 m and single beam crane capacity not exceeding 5 tons.
	5.	Light industrial buildings and warehouses with spans not exceeding 15 m and not exceeding 3 storeys.
	6.	Medium-sized and small chimneys, water towers and tanks to be designed with the use of standardized drawings.
		All construction projects to be designed by design institutes of Group D should not contain basements.

There are three types of ownership for construction companies in China.

First, state-owned enterprises under the state budget are enterprises under direct management of the financial budget of the government. They are well equipped with construction plant for the construction of complex projects, for example, the Metallurgy Construction Company No. 20, which built the Baoshan Iron and Steel Complex. They might also be construction companies that are owned by ministries, for example, the Ministry of Railways' various construction companies, whose annual work output in 1988, Rmb¥6.7 billion, represented about 9% of the total output of state-owned construction companies.

Second, collective-owned enterprises owned by the people as a whole and not under the state budget (but in reality owned by the state). For instance, the provinces, municipalities and cities have local construction corporations that report directly to the local construction commissions. A construction corporation oversees a number of construction companies within its municipality and is responsible for allocating resources to them. The role of the corporations is to co-ordinate the work of the companies under their control. They are also responsible for various building-associated organizations, such as component manufacturers. The nearest Western equivalent for a construction corporation would be a holding company. For example, the Shanghai Municipal Construction Commission oversees the Shanghai Building Construction Corporation which, in turn, comprises six construction companies.

Third, true collective ownership of construction companies through rural construction teams, although an increasing amount of work is being undertaken by collective-owned enterprises in the urban areas. The means of production are collectively owned by the workers. Rural construction teams can be run by villages, cities, towns and neighbourhood committees. This sector has grown rapidly since 1982. It operates almost entirely outside the state planning system.

In 1988, there were nearly 19,000,000 workers and staff members employed by 87,224 construction enterprises of whom:

- 6,235,000 work in 3,798 state-owned enterprises
- 4,213,000 work in 10,336 collective-owned enterprises in cities and towns; and
- 8,546,000 work in 73,090 rural construction teams.

Although rural construction teams represent a large percentage of the total number engaged in construction, they are made up of small groups of people building housing and other small simple projects for the local community with limited plant and equipment. They tend not to have highly skilled engineering staff, indeed many of their workers are unskilled and work mainly on the land. Sometimes they act as sub-contractors on major projects, for example, building workers' housing on a large factory project.

The larger construction companies employ as many as 25,000 people and work on major construction projects. In 1988 the total output of state-owned construction companies alone was over Rmb¥77 billion.

Within this framework, construction companies are licensed and classified into four categories in terms of the size of projects that they are allowed to construct. Classification is based upon their fixed assets, expertise and previous experience. Apart from the national contractors, they will normally undertake work only in the municipality or province to which they belong. They may, however, work in other regions, but need to obtain permission from construction commissions in the areas in which they wish to work. Permission to work overseas can be given only by state authorities.

One contractor in the PRC dwarfs all others, both in turnover and the number of people it employs. The China State Construction Engineering Corporation (CSCEC) employs nearly 190,000 people. It is organized into 59 construction enterprises and undertakes large projects anywhere in the PRC. As well as working in particular regions, each of the companies specializes in either civil engineering work or building construction. Two of the CSCEC subsidiaries, the Garden Construction Company and the Chang Chang Construction Company, have built many notable buildings in Beijing.

The CSCEC also has an overseas division which has been involved in 400 overseas projects in 50 countries. For the Hong Kong subsidiary alone, production and investment was over HK$9.5 billion between 1979–89. It accounts for about one-third of the services provided by China's overseas construction and labour services companies.

Foreign general contractors are rarely employed on indigenous projects unless they have some special technology to offer because:

- China wishes to maximize and develop the use of its own labour and skills;
- foreign contractors have higher operating costs that, in general, result in their prices or tenders being higher than those submitted by indigenous companies; and
- foreign companies will be paid in Renminbi for local projects. The currency is not internationally convertible.

The Cost

The *China Statistical Yearbooks* appear to be the only source of prices for indigenous projects. Table 3.4 shows the costs of various types of project. All prices quoted are in Rmb¥/m^2, are exclusive of land cost and no account is taken of regional price differences.

The prices are incompatible with prices for joint venture projects. Also, they appear inconsistent across various building types, but this cannot be analysed as the basis of the statistics is not known.

Table 3.4

Unit cost of completed buildings through capital construction.

Year	Average of all types of buildings	Factories	Ware-houses	Office buildings	Residential buildings	School buildings	Buildings for medical purposes	Other buildings
1957	56	102	42	59	47	51	70	58
1965	81	140	71	71	59	70	85	77
1978	104	153	92	98	89	79	103	100
1980	123	173	111	118	113	106	134	137
1982	147	206	136	142	135	138	167	176
1984	187	282	182	185	160	163	224	246
1986	231	340	224	245	196	208	248	310
1987	270	378	260	280	213	227	293	378
1988	301	423	269	310	241	251	330	410

(Rmb¥/m²)

Source: China Statistical Yearbook 1989
Note: Excluding land cost, demolishing and removal expenses and investment in outdoor supplementary projects.

JOINT VENTURE PROJECTS

The normal procedure within the PRC is for Party A (the PRC party or parties) and Party B (the foreign party or parties) to form a foreign investment joint venture company to agree upon and appoint representatives to an internal and separate joint venture board to deal with and co-ordinate construction projects required in connection with the joint venture. The expertise and experience of the parties either in the field of construction or development will determine whether the joint venture board will provide the management and co-ordination roles within the project structure.

If the joint venture board is familiar with construction projects and the task of co-ordinating and managing the many parties that are involved, then the board may do this using its own resources. This may take the form of a preparatory office to co-ordinate the project with or without any independent project management organization being involved.

If, however, the joint venture company is relatively inexperienced with construction projects, the board may appoint a company to manage the project on its behalf. Such an outside company could be a foreign project management company, construction company, or design practice.

Figure 3.4 illustrates an example of organization structure that might be used for a construction project, but it is stressed that there are a wide range of arrangements available to suit particular circumstances of each project.

Whilst preparatory offices are not mandatory on joint venture projects they may be used as an extension of the local construction system. In such cases they are established jointly by Party A and Party B. Often, Party A will supply the manager and Party B the deputy manager. The deputy manager may be based outside China and only visit, say, twice a month. The use of a preparatory office does not mean that there will not be a project manager also employed by Party B. If there was, the project manager would work in conjunction with the preparatory office. Preparatory offices have been known to have up to 300 staff depending on the size of the project.

Construction companies normally rely on design institutes and foreign designers for designing to a shop drawing level of detail for all aspects of the work to be constructed. Larger construction companies, however, are beginning to provide some drawings for some joint venture projects. Operational drawings, showing location of plant and sequence of working, may also be produced by contractors.

The process of tendering is common to both indigenous and joint venture projects. The client can select the construction companies that may tender.

A Tender Management Office exists in each local government region, which ensures that both the client and contractor are qualified to undertake the work. It consists of representatives from each local government department with an interest in construction, for example, the local construction commission and the People's Construction Bank.

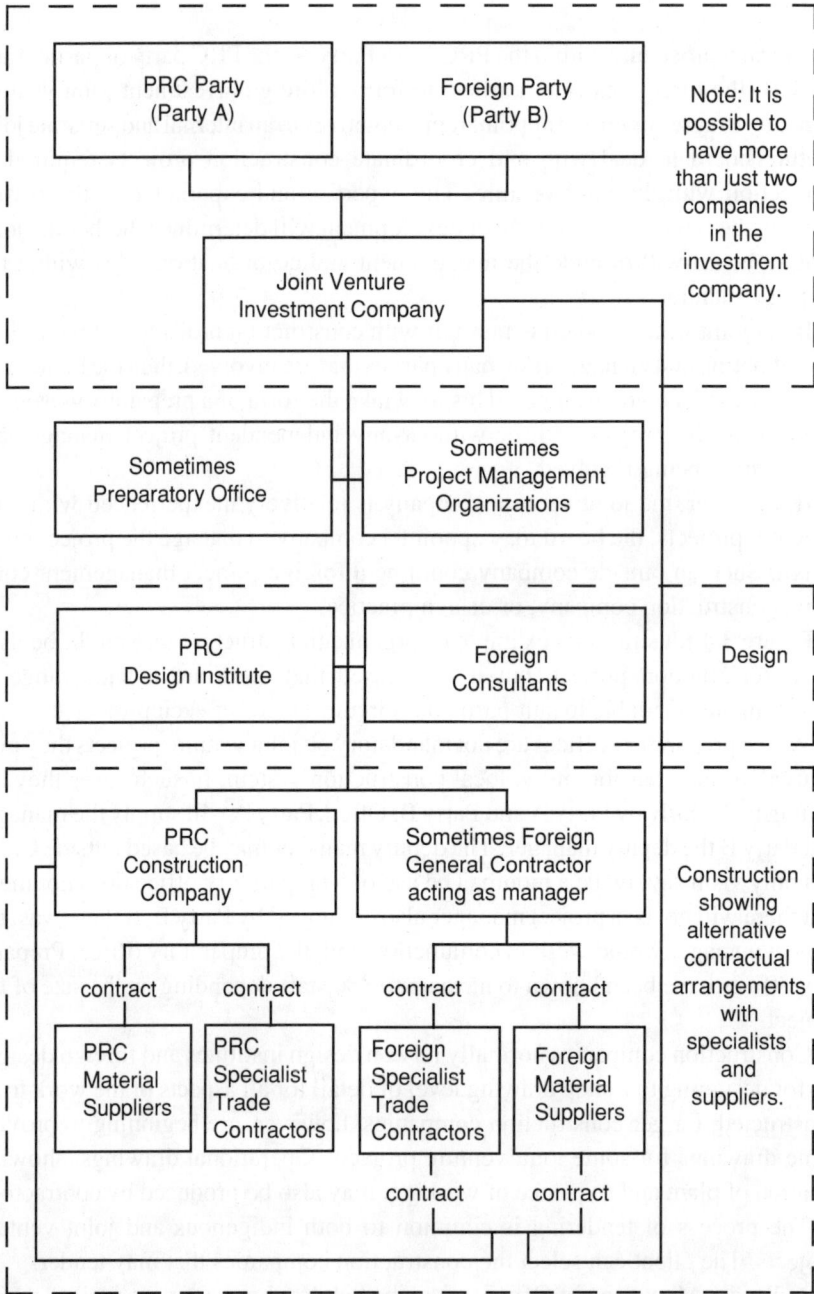

Fig. 3.4 An example of organization structure for a construction project.

When qualifying the client, it considers such things as whether the client has financial resources, available land and ability to prepare tender documentation and monitor construction.

When selecting the contractor, the client joins the group and essentially decides which contractor shall be awarded the contract. The representatives from local government are there principally to make sure their rules are followed. The objective is to ensure that the contractor chosen is qualified to construct the scale and complexity of the project under consideration.

On joint venture projects the liability for latent defects can be a problem. The joint venture client and owner of the building will be Chinese and one or more overseas parties; the user could be, for example, a Japanese hotel corporation or bank. The design team may comprise a Chinese design institute, with an American architect, a British structural engineer and a Hong Kong mechanical and electrical engineer. The contractor will more than likely be Chinese, but the specialist trade contractors and the product manufacturers will come from various overseas countries.

The Approval Procedure

The PRC's complex state administration system can present formidable problems for foreign joint venture partners contemplating investment in construction. However, there are indications that organization of the process is improving and that there are more workable regulations. In Hainan, it is said that the Ministry of Foreign Economic Relations and Trade (MOFERT) co-ordinates all agencies in the process.

The diagram presented in Figure 3.5 shows a simplified view of the process of obtaining investment and capital construction approvals. The approval procedures may vary from locality to locality and project to project.

Investment approvals and construction approvals are both part of the same process. A more detailed account of the procedures and the contents of associated feasibility studies is given in *China: Building for Joint Ventures*, published by Levett and Bailey.

Designing the Project

It is mandatory for a foreign architectural and engineering design practice to work in conjunction with a design institute. Hence, the joint venture company has two options for arranging design:

- the employment of a foreign design practice working in collaboration with a PRC design institute or vice versa; or
- the employment of a local PRC design institute.

National planning	Approvals	Process	Costs
National economic development plan	Should fit within the plan	Partners deliberate on Joint Venture project	
	Examined and approved by LPC/SPC	Preparation of project proposal report	Preliminary estimate
Long-term capital construction plan	Examined and approved by LPC/SPC	Preliminary and/or joint feasibility study	Investment estimate
	Examined and approved by MOFERT or local FERTC	Joint Venture contract agreement	
	Approved by SAIC or local Bureau	Application for business registration and licence	
		Open an account with BOC and other appropriate banks and register with local Tax Bureau	
		Payment of investment funds to BOC	
	Approved by local land administration bureau	Application for land use certificate	
		Very latest time for formally appointing Project Management Group (if used) and latest time for formally appointing Design Team	
Annual capital construction plan	Examined and approved by LEC & LCC	Design	Approximate design estimate
		Technical design/ working drawings and tender documents	Detailed design estimate or target cost
	Tender approved by TMO	Appoint/Tender Construction	
		Construction progress	Interim progress payments
		Construction completion and handover	Final account

FERTC
Foreign Economic Relations and Trade Commissions

LCC
Local Construction Commission

LEC
Local Economic Commission

LPC
Local Planning Commission

MOFERT
Ministry of Foreign Economic Relations and Trade

SAIC
State Administration of Industry and Commerce

SPC
State Planning Commission

BOC
Bank of China

TMO
Tender Management Office

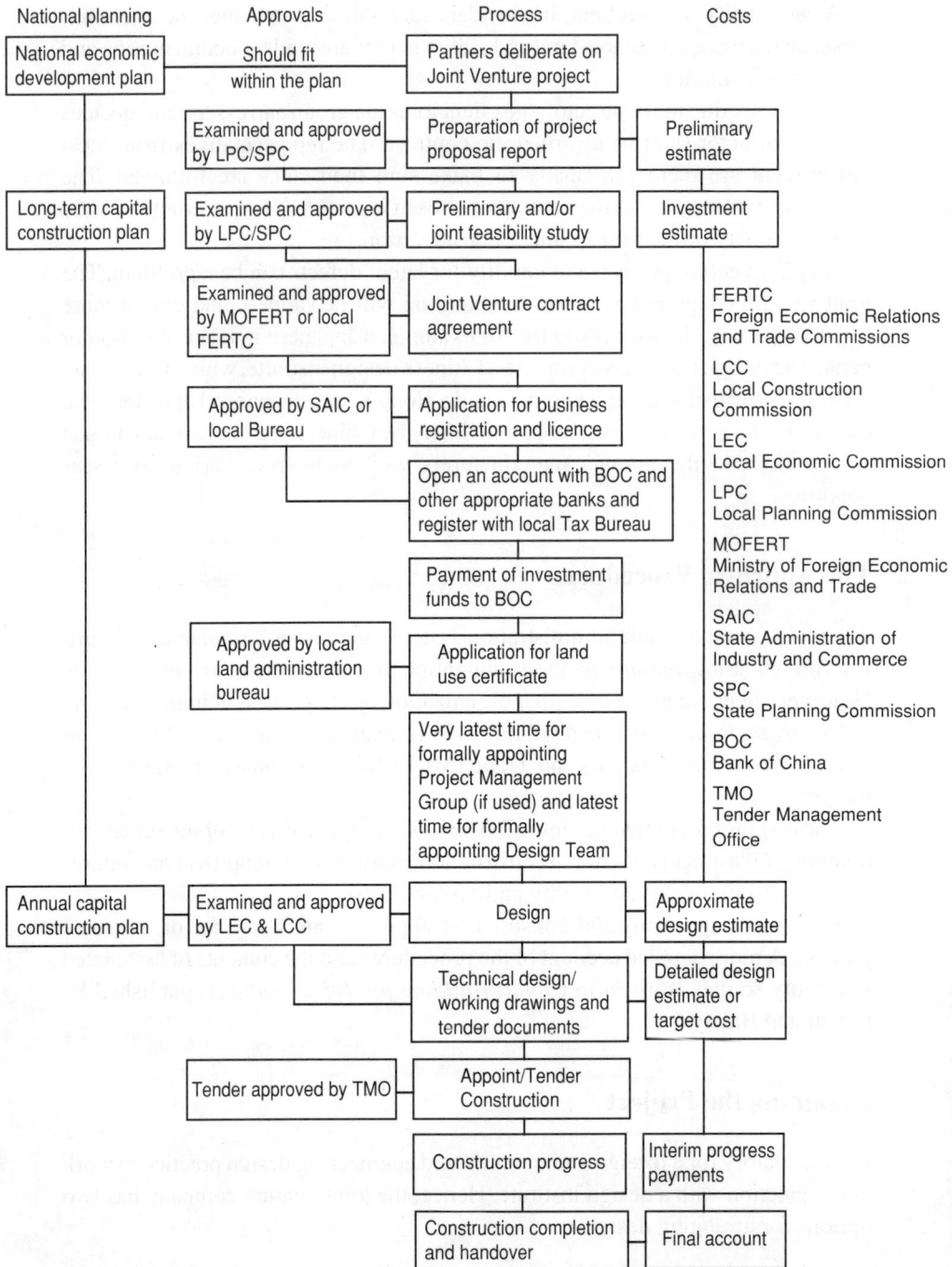

Fig. 3.5 Investment and capital construction approval procedures.

Foreign investors will feel comfortable dealing with a design team with which they are familiar and can more easily communicate. Nevertheless, an American, or a British, German, or Japanese architect or engineer, despite having an international reputation for design and innovation, will require the assistance, collaboration and advice of a PRC design institute that is experienced in designing and administering projects in the PRC. A major difficulty is the language problem. Obviously all working documents must be in Chinese.

Collaboration on design is successful as both parties have something to gain. Design institutes gain experience of advanced building technology such as mechanical and electrical engineering installations, sophisticated curtain wall systems; in short, technology transfer. The foreign design practices gain a pathfinder through the bureaucracy. The specific benefits of working in this way are that the PRC design institute will:

- understand the complex planning and building approval processes and steer the design through them;
- provide information on city planning requirements such as height restrictions and zoning;
- provide information on gas, water, telephone and electrical utilities;
- be familiar with local building regulations and specification requirements;
- have knowledge of the frequent amendments to the various regulations and approval processes and advise on their implementation;
- know the level of design details required to be supplied to the construction companies;
- be able to assist in translating any documentation;
- be familiar with local trade and site practices;
- know of the availability of local materials; and
- be able to provide the appropriate level of contacts in other government agencies.

Allocation of Design Institutes to Joint Venture Projects

The normal procedure is for the construction commission to allocate a design institute to a foreign design team. A number of design institutes have built up a working relationship with foreign teams, and in these circumstances the foreign design teams can request that they work with a particular design institute. In other cases, Party A has knowledge of the design institutes and can arrange for a specific one to be allocated.

Design Details Required

The amount of design details necessary for construction companies in China is much greater than that normally expected in the West. Design drawings will be to a fine level of details; in most instances, down to the level of detail of shop drawings showing exactly how each of the items is to be fabricated and fixed. Complete detailed drawings are also required for tendering purposes. The construction commissions issue rules regarding the amount of design details to be provided at each approval stage.

It is not uncommon for technical exchange meetings to be held between design institute, overseas designers and the appointed construction companies (or all prospective tenderers when competitive tendering is to be used) to discuss the design and detailing.

Collaboration between Foreign Design Teams and Design Institutes

The extent to which design institutes become involved in the design process of joint ventures varies considerably depending upon their individual initiative, motivation and abilities.

Initially, the foreign designers decided how far the design institutes became involved. There were essentially two levels, either technical consultation to ensure regulations were satisfied, or co-operation design which involved much closer involvement with the design institute. The details of who does what are negotiated between the two parties. The co-operation design approach is now rapidly becoming the required approach, as design institutes increasingly wish to become more closely involved in design as their experience of joint ventures develops, with the eventual aim of working alone. The principal areas in which design institutes will need to develop their knowledge base for this to happen are with sophisticated mechanical and electrical service installations, and with 'high tech' finishes both internally and externally. There will also need to be an increasing awareness of quality and a change in attitude towards quality assurance and quality control.

Design Approvals and Presentations

A project goes through four approval processes with presentations made at each stage. The PRC does not have the equivalent of the Royal Institute of British Architects plan of work or the American Institute of Architects guidelines for architectural and engineering services, so there is no standardized terminology for the design phases. Names of the actual stages and amount of details required at each stage differ between local government regions. Generally, the four stages are:

- feasibility;
- conceptual design;
- preliminary design;
- detailed design.

In certain circumstances, such as a tight programme, simplicity of the project or experience of the designers, these stages may be reduced. It is not uncommon for the conceptual and preliminary design stages to be combined into one extended preliminary design stage or even for the feasibility and conceptual design stages to be combined.

Feasibility

Normally outline design drawings are required together with a detailed appraisal. A number of optional proposals are usual at this stage, each accompanied by an economic appraisal. The Chinese system is very democratic and requires formal presentations to be made to all relevant authorities and departments, who will choose the most appropriate scheme. The audience could include senior local authority representatives such as local planning department, mayor, deputy mayor and general secretary of the local government region. Groups of fifty or sixty people are not uncommon.

Conceptual Design

This stage is rather more than conceptual. It is equivalent to what is often referred to in other countries as schematic design, but the focus is on design approach, meeting town planning requirements and cultural requirements. A set of quite well developed drawings that show the scope and standard of the project, including architectural design, interior design, structural design and mechanical and electrical services are usually required.

The proposals at this stage are also presented formally before an audience which can be as large as one hundred people. Those who are eligible to attend include representatives of the public utilities, transportation, town planning, police, fire services and anyone else who is affected by or interested in the project.

The designers are expected to take notice of the points of criticism made by the audience, but the design institute can often advise on which comments have to be incorporated and which may be disregarded. The design institute can also assist in identifying those changes that would overcome the criticisms.

Preliminary Design

This stage is more detailed than would be expected for a preliminary design submission in other countries. The level of detail required is similar to that expected for the equivalent of building regulation approval elsewhere, including all calculations and building services design.

Again, presentation takes place before a large audience, as at the conceptual stage but with the addition of all tendering construction companies. Some members of the audience check that the concept has not changed, others will be concerned with ensuring regulations are being complied with. The construction companies may suggest changes, which may have to be taken into account; these are often influenced by what form of construction the construction companies prefer to build. Assistance is available from the design institute in resolving any difficulties and, as mentioned earlier, the authorities are now tending to favour the designer's view.

Detailed Design

This stage is equivalent to the production of working drawings and shop drawings. This extends, for example, to details of all pipe service runs including the spacing and method of pipe fixings. It reflects the requirements of the construction companies to have drawings at a fine level of detail before tendering, although in practice tendering often takes place before this level of detail has been developed.

The need for this stage varies considerably between regions. It may be combined with the preliminary design stage if drawings are sufficiently well developed.

Approval of this stage is permission to build.

Co-ordination and Decision Making

Co-ordination demands are high on joint venture projects. They are needed not only between the foreign and PRC designers, but also between the various parties within the PRC.

The use of a project manager, resident co-ordinating architect, or construction manager for both design and construction co-ordination and supervision is likely to be beneficial. The co-ordination needs in the PRC appear to be considerably greater than for comparable projects in many other countries. It is just as important in the PRC as elsewhere to establish professional relationships at all levels in order to work in a climate of confidence and respect.

The decision making process in the PRC can be more consultative than that normally experienced by the foreign parties. Chinese foreign investors, developers and consultants have a distinct advantage over other nationalities being familiar with the language and culture. This is one of the reasons why a large proportion of investment in joint ventures in the PRC is channelled through Hong Kong.

In the hierarchical structure of the PRC, only senior members make decisions and the foreign parties therefore have to have someone of equally senior rank involved, even in the case of relatively minor decisions. This can be most demanding on the time of senior executives and partners.

Standard Specifications

There are no comprehensive nationally approved standard specifications for construction work, but there are locally approved standards. Those that do exist are mainly structural, others are in the process of being developed. Each local government region has its own standards issued by the construction commissions, which are being continually revised. The rate of development varies between regions and frequently overseas standards, for example, Japanese and USA, are used.

Construction Cost Advice

Specialist foreign consultants are frequently employed to manage and control construction cost from inception through to completion. Cost control is vitally important to the joint venture parties, the PRC authorities and the banks. As a result, quantity surveying and cost engineering practices are employed for cost management on many joint venture projects.

Constructing the Project

The PRC has strict rules about involvement of foreign general contractors in its construction industry. Foreign general contractors work mainly on some foreign investment joint ventures, foreign aid projects, World Bank and special high technology turnkey projects such as power stations or chemical plants. Increasingly foreign general contractors are discouraged from undertaking foreign investment joint venture projects in order to provide local construction companies with opportunities to construct them.

The same discouragement does not apply to foreign specialist contractors, which are encouraged for technology transfer. Foreign general contractors often act in a management role only, for similar reasons.

For a joint venture company that needs to build, there are normally three options available for construction:

- the employment of a PRC construction company or a number of companies undertaking different sections of the project;
- the employment of a PRC construction company together with a foreign construction company, which acts in a management role only; or
- the employment of a PRC construction company together with a foreign construction company in a joint venture construction company.

A preparatory office may be used as the co-ordinator when a number of separate PRC construction companies are employed for different sections of the work and even when one acts as the general contractor. Alternatively a foreign project management organization may be used, which could be part of an overseas contractors organization.

The major construction corporations that can be expected to work on foreign investment projects are owned by either the state, province or municipality. Construction corporations administer and are responsible for overseeing the work of construction companies under their control. These may include specialist contractors such as building engineering services contractors, often referred to as engineering installation contractors.

The client selects a contractor to construct the project. This may be by selecting one contractor and negotiating a price or by tendering. In the latter case the client selects the list of tenderers. Normally Party A will have a sound knowledge of construction companies available or is in a position to obtain information. Although the construction commission's approval to appointing a particular contractor does not appear to be necessary, it is advisable to keep them informed.

Construction can be organized in collaboration with a foreign construction company with whom the PRC construction company enters into an agreement. Generally, this option is allowed only when advanced technical and managerial skills are required for major complex joint venture projects such as nuclear power stations.

Even if it was generally allowed, it would be impracticable for a foreign general contractor to work in the PRC without the collaboration of a PRC construction company because of the problems encountered in obtaining local labour and materials and in dealing with the many parties and government agencies involved. Hence, in many cases, foreign general contractors provide a project management service only, when working with a Chinese construction company.

However, in rare cases when foreign general contractors have been employed independently in the PRC, most frequently on 'high tech' turnkey projects, the contractor has some form of equity participation. There remain exceptions to the discouragement of foreign general contractors. For instance, the China World Trade Centre joint venture project in Beijing is a US$231 million hotel, office and apartment complex, which was awarded to a leading French general contractor, Societe Auxiliare d'Entreprises (SAE). One of the obligations of the contractor is to employ Chinese workers and provide technical training to the Chinese specialist trade contractors.

The situation varies considerably between regions. For instance, the administration in Beijing is considered to be rigid whereas foreign contractors are actually registered contractors in Shenzhen, although the registration was done many years ago.

Sub-contracting

Work may be locally sub-contracted for piling, decorating and simple engineering services. The sub-contractors could be one of the units comprising the same construction corporation as the general contractor, but the general contractor will contract with them directly.

Foreign sub-contractors are used for high technology aspects of construction with which PRC companies and workers are unfamiliar. Examples such as structural steel frames, glazed external cladding, complex mechanical services and high quality internal finishing are now common features of joint venture construction projects. The PRC welcomes this sort of technology advancement in construction and has been keen to allow foreign specialist contractors and suppliers to work with PRC contractors to achieve technology transfer. In this arrangement the foreign specialists are usually employed directly by the joint venture company.

The foreign sub-contractor may provide imported labour, materials and equipment to carry out his work; in other cases some resources may be provided locally. Labour may be a local resource and this aids the technology transfer process. The foreign sub-contractor's role is to develop the design through to shop drawings in liaison with the main design team, manufacture or supply the system concerned, and provide site supervision.

The PRC workers frequently function as 'labour only' sub-contractors. For example, on a project in the PRC, the structural steel frame was supplied from Japan, welding and fabrication of the frame was then carried out by the Chinese sub-contractor under direct supervision of the Japanese supplier. In such cases quality control and programming is the responsibility of the foreign specialist company. The construction companies also become involved in such arrangements and technical staff from the companies work alongside the foreign specialist staff to learn the different construction techniques and quality control procedures. Figure 3.6 shows a possible role of foreign specialist sub-contractors in a joint venture project.

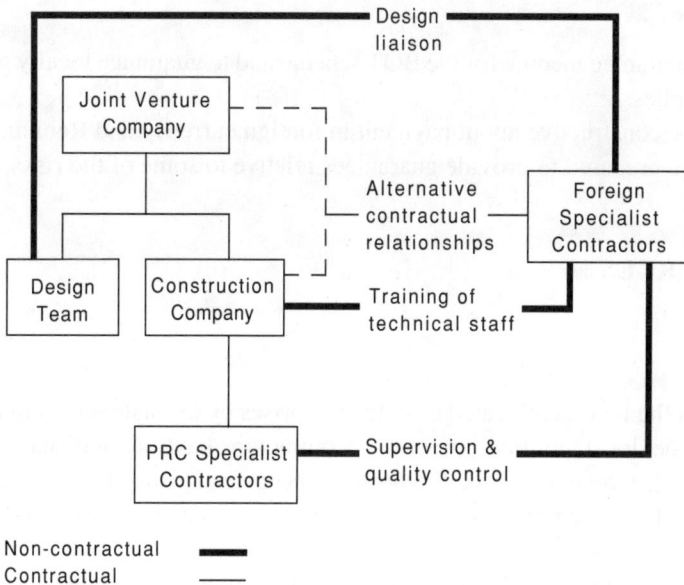

Fig. 3.6 The interaction of foreign specialist contractors.

Build–Operate–Transfer

Build–Operate–Transfer (BOT) schemes have great attraction to the PRC and, if structured properly, are advantageous to the investors. China hopes to attract this type of operation for major infrastructure development such as roads, bridges, ports and energy. The major benefit to the PRC is that the foreign investor is totally responsible for funding and accepts one-point responsibility for the scheme, and technology transfer takes place during both construction and operation before the project is handed to China.

Hopewell's experience with the Shajiao Power Station described earlier can be used to generalize the aspects of BOT schemes that contribute to their success:

For the foreign party

- spending a great deal of time understanding the Chinese situation and gaining their trust;
- not being there just to sell consulting expertise, equipment, or the latest state of the arts but to contribute to China's modernization;
- willingness to put up, and potentially lose, equity investment if the project falters or fails;
- agreeing to bring in the capital required for the project;
- to give the facility to China at no cost at the end of the co-operation period.

For China

- to guarantee income for the BOT scheme and to guarantee locally produced supplies.
- to be constructive about payment in foreign currency and Renminbi;
- to be prepared to provide guarantees relative to some of the risks.

RESOURCES

Labour

Labour in the PRC is allocated to state enterprises by the state on a quota system through the local political structure. Contractors have skilled and unskilled construction workers and staff who have been technically trained, mainly as engineers. Both men and women are employed as construction workers and as staff.

The PRC does not have unemployment; the Constitution guarantees everybody's right to work. The state allocates the person to a task commensurate with his or her skills. 'Daiye' (waiting for work) is not classified as unemployed.

There are three basic types of construction worker:

- permanent worker;
- contract worker;
- temporary worker.

Permanent workers include staff, skilled and semi-skilled operatives, and apprentices in all trades. Permanent employees do not normally move from company to company unless directed by the state as they may lose social benefits.

Contract workers are usually on 1, 2, or 3 years contracts and have a good chance of becoming permanent. This form of employment is being encouraged at present. Such workers do not receive all the benefits of permanent workers.

Temporary workers are employed for short durations. They have no contract with the construction companies and are paid a daily rate. They generally make up the majority of semi-skilled and unskilled workers. They are usually recruited from the countryside where there is an excess of labour due to greater efficiency in farming.

Technical staff are responsible for providing technical support to management and include planning, estimating and materials engineers, as well as structural engineers, building services engineers and site surveyors.

The construction companies have responsibility for the welfare of the workers and staff. These may include aspects such as catering, housing, education and nursery services.

Bonuses

An incentive-based bonus (or responsibility) scheme is used in the PRC construction industry as an incentive for more efficient work. The incentive for technical and administrative staff is an enhancement of their promotion prospects, grade and status.

The bonus schemes can be divided into two types:

- trade bonus schemes;
- project bonus schemes.

Trade Bonus Schemes

These are assessed for each individual trade. The criteria used to assess the bonus are mainly: early completion of the work, quality of the finished product and cost savings in the use of building materials.

On joint venture projects where a bonus applies, about 15% of the project cost is allocated to wages and bonus. The bonus quota is allocated 50% to the workers and 50% to the construction company.

Project Bonus Schemes

This is an 'ahead of schedule' bonus and, if it is required, the terms and conditions of its payment should be negotiated before a contract is signed. The project bonus is paid to the construction company, which retains part and passes part to the state.

Materials and Plant

Chinese Building Materials

Through the system of central planning, the state has controlled supplies of raw materials and manufactured goods to the construction industry. In the past China has not had builders' merchants. Materials have come directly from manufacturers and have been allocated at either state or local level.

In an attempt to rationalize supplies, a new development in major cities has been the introduction of building materials trading centres, in essence, state-controlled builders' merchants. The trading centres obtain supplies from state manufacturers who produce above the state quotas.

Although in recent years output of building materials has increased sharply, supply of important materials such as cement, timber and steel reinforcement has been inadequate as demand outstripped supply. Since the economic slow down and the political unrest, materials have become more readily available and the prices have been reduced.

The PRC produces few modern lightweight building materials, but products such as extruded aluminium for windows and doors are now being produced. The quality of products such as tiles, ceiling materials, marble and granite have been improving over recent years.

Building materials can be classified in the following ways:

- centrally managed materials such as cement, steel, glass and timber, which are controlled and provided for distribution throughout the PRC by the state;
- regionally managed materials, for example, bricks, stone, sand and aggregates, which are usually produced and consumed within one district and controlled by the province, city, or municipality Bureau for Building Materials;
- market materials such as door locks, light bulbs, which have little influence on the national economy, are sold on the open market with a certain amount of price competition. Quantities of materials that are above the factory quotas are also sold outside the central planning system on the market. Such sales include all major materials.

The source of materials varies from project to project depending upon the project's status. For example, a top priority project may have 100% of materials supplied by the State or local Bureau for Building Materials; a second priority project may have only 80% allocated, a third priority project 50–60% and so on. Some projects may not receive any allocation. The balance of materials has to be obtained on the open market outside the state planning system.

Imported Building Materials

In the case of a joint venture project, the joint venture board would normally be responsible for the procurement of all foreign materials and would initially have to apply to the State Bureau for Building Materials for permission. Once permission is granted the joint venture board will contract directly with foreign manufacturers and suppliers.

When applying for permission to import materials, a comprehensive and detailed list with quantities is needed early in the design process if delays are to be avoided. No list of permitted imported materials exists and generally any material may now be imported for joint venture projects. The list should include names of the suppliers and sub-contractors involved.

Import duly will have to be paid, although it is waived in the economic zones and in some other circumstances for joint venture projects. China has a two tiered tariff system: Most Favoured Nation (MFN) and ordinary rates. If MFN status has been granted, then there are reductions in ordinary tariff rates.

The import of materials that are also manufactured in the PRC is controlled by quotas. The quotas apply to an administrative district. For example, the Shenzhen SEZ can import only 10,000 tons of steel a month.

Plant and Equipment

Although the PRC produces a range of construction plant, the variety and quantity is still limited and China is not yet able to meet the increasing demands for mechanized methods of working.

Construction plant purchased from foreign manufacturers is therefore imported for indigenous projects, but is tightly controlled. Application must be made through local construction commission, by which the transaction, if it is approved, will be carried out. Normally only plant not manufactured within China may be imported for use on local projects.

As with building materials, construction plant and equipment manufactured in China is centrally controlled and planned through provincial and municipal construction commissions. Central planning is, however, concerned only with larger items of plant and equipment, and many smaller items may be purchased directly by construction companies without having to apply to their provincial or municipal committee.

Joint venture projects may, however, import any type of plant provided appropriate approvals are obtained. Import duty and tax may be payable on imported vehicles and plant if they are not re-exported after use.

CONTRACTS AND COSTS

Contracts

PRC Forms of Contract

The PRC does not have standard forms of contract for construction, but the government issues guidelines, which are adapted for local use.

Cultural differences can be seen clearly in the PRC attitude to construction contracts. The PRC contract envisages the two parties working together in a spirit of co-operation and equality, using their best endeavours to carry out the State's construction project efficiently and economically. Documents are characterized by the distinctly non-legalistic term — 'all items not found in this contract will be deliberated and decided upon in a spirit of mutual understanding and trust'.

However, the PRC government are preparing a contract based on F.I.D.I.C. for use nationally, but this is not yet completed.

Foreign Forms of Contracts

Foreign investors will feel comfortable working with building contract conditions with which they are familiar: it might be F.I.D.I.C. or American or Japanese standard forms. Use of the Hong Kong standard form of building contract, which is based upon standard British forms, is widespread on joint venture projects that involve Hong Kong parties. In all cases it is normal to modify foreign standard forms to comply with local conditions, for example, method of payment.

Similarly, the Hong Kong standard nominated sub-contract form is frequently used with adaptation for contracts between general contractors and foreign specialist trade contractors. However, foreign specialist trade contractors often contract directly with the joint venture client and not with the general contractor, and special contracts have to be devised for such circumstances. Sometimes contracts for major specialist installations are signed by the client, general contractor and specialist trade contractors. These are known as 'three party contracts' and payments are made directly by the client to the specialist trade contractors.

Speed, Quality and Costs

Speed of Construction

There is little doubt that possible delays during construction are a major concern to both indigenous and joint venture clients, but this is not necessarily worse than for many other countries. It is accepted that the PRC can build quickly when there is no external delaying factor. Delays occur when construction is suspended or interfered with for a number of factors of which the following are common:

- shortage of materials;
- poor maintenance, inappropriate selection and uninformed use of equipment;
- weak co-ordination of mechanical and electrical engineering services;
- too high a level of decision making;
- inexperienced site management;
- late connection to utilities; and
- inappropriate allocation of labour.

Quality

The achievement of quality standards similar to those expected of an international project is difficult in the PRC. It requires constant vigilance and attention to details as the indigenous construction industry does not have the tradition of producing work of such a quality. However, good quality can be achieved and improvements have been rapid. Evidence of high quality local work can be seen in renovations of vernacular buildings.

Construction Costs in Perspective

Lack of published data and limited experience of foreign companies operating in the PRC generate many misconceptions about building costs in the PRC Daily labour wage rates are low compared with many industrial nations, but this does not mean that construction costs on joint venture projects will be very low. The prices for joint venture projects are not local PRC construction prices paid by local Chinese clients. These are lower because of government subsidies, which are not allowed to foreign joint venture clients.

In addition, overseas investors are building particular types of buildings, mainly hotels, apartment buildings, factories, process plants and office buildings, whereas everyday construction in the PRC predominantly involves different classes of buildings such as housing, schools, railways, hospitals and so on. Very different technology and materials are used in the PRC for building 'international standard' projects than for most indigenous construction projects.

To put PRC construction prices into perspective, Table 3.5 shows construction prices for hotels and factories in certain cities in selected countries throughout the world. The prices are only intended to be broadly indicative and cities have been given due to regional variations within countries. The PRC prices refer to joint venture projects using foreign investment.

Table 3.5 shows that the Hong Kong and the PRC construction prices are very close. The special geographic and economic relationships of Hong Kong and the PRC have a strong influence.

Table 3.5
International construction prices.

Country	Currency	Hotel construction price range/m^2 (a)	Factory construction price range/m^2 (b)
People's Republic of China (Shanghai)	Renminbi Yuan	Rmb¥5,500–8,500	Rmb¥1,500–1,800
Hong Kong	Hong Kong Dollar	HK$10,000–14,000	HK$2,500–3,000
United States of America (San Francisco)	US Dollar	US$1,500–1,800	US$450–800
Australia (Sydney)	Australian Dollar	A$2,500–3,000	A$530–800
United Kingdom (London)	Sterling	£1,100–1,500	£350–550
Japan (Tokyo)	Yen	¥600,000–800,000	¥150,000–250,000

Notes: (a) Based upon a five-star international class hotel including furnishing, furniture and equipment at June 1990 price levels.
  (b) Based upon a light industrial shed approximately 10,000 m^2 superficial area of owner occupation at June 1990 price levels.
  (c) Prices do not include local taxes in the USA.
  (d) Prices are exclusive of land cost and professional fees.
  (e) Shanghai is located in an area of river silt, which can be more than 150 m deep. The foundation costs are substantially higher than for cities such as Beijing.

Special Features of Construction Costs

There is no standard pricing system for joint venture projects and consequently prices are arrived by competitive tendering or negotiation with contractors.

The following factors will have an influence upon prices.

• Daily wage rates must not be taken at face value. A monthly basic wage for a general labourer working for a construction company may be Rmb¥60 and is approximately double for a senior skilled craftsman; additionally a bonus of Rmb¥30–40 per month may be earned. Construction workers will also receive subsidized housing, which costs them no more than Rmb¥15 a month (the size of the house is dependent upon the status of the worker), free health care for himself and his family, free schooling for his children, a pension upon retirement, money for certain rations. All these benefits are provided by the state through the construction company. Therefore, when calculating a day rate for a PRC operative working on a foreign investment joint venture project, the wage rate must be adjusted to reflect the 'real cost'. Construction companies will normally charge a joint venture company a basic rate of between US$6–15 per day for labour exclusive of indirect costs, but the rate charged has been known to be as high as US$20–30 per day. The Chinese will maintain that this is the economic value of labour, i.e., Chinese labour is no cheaper than other labour and the price has to include all the welfare benefits provided by the state. The rates quoted and strength in negotiation often depends upon the PRC joint venture partner's influence. Productivity becomes important at these rates.

- Productivity, measured as the output per hour per worker, is not simply a factor of skill and commitment of the building workers as it is greatly influenced by mechanization, technology, incentive schemes and management. The average productivity per hour for Chinese building workers can be significantly less than those of the industrialized countries. The shortfall is made up by using many more manual workers who work long hours for six days a week. Chinese contractors are quite prepared to work a shift system for a 24-hour day programme at a premium, which would be negotiable.
- Construction companies try to negotiate an ahead-of-schedule bonus from joint venture companies whenever possible.
- The state recognizes that there are regional influences on prices, and workers' wages are weighted according to the region where they are employed.
- Under Article 53 of China's Constitution, men and women enjoy equal pay for equal work. Many of China's construction workers are women.
- China, especially the north and north-east regions, is subject to earthquakes. Special foundations and structural frames are required to minimize the earthquake effects on buildings.
- Western construction technology is not the same as traditional Chinese construction technology. High-rise building is not common, but is increasing in popularity. China does not have an abundance of timber so consequently steel forms and pre-cast concrete components are used extensively. The slipform process of concreting is being used on some projects in the major cities.
- The state controls the labour, materials and equipment used on a project.
- The PRC gives priority to joint venture projects for the supply of PRC produced materials and when a joint venture is approved, a licence is granted for materials. Any materials can now be imported for joint venture projects, but in each case a licence is required.
- A major problem faced by PRC construction companies is a lack of working

capital, especially in foreign currency, for joint venture projects. As a reflection of this problem, contractors may require the provision of an initial advance payment as a term of the contract.

- Competitive tendering is encouraged by the Central Government for both indigenous and joint venture projects and contractors are sometimes allowed to tender for work outside their province or normal sphere of activity. However, in areas such as the major cities, if the amount of construction activities places a heavy demand upon the contractors, it is not always practical to obtain tenders. It may be necessary to negotiate with one selected contractor.

- Inflation of building costs is a natural corollary to general inflation, which has been a factor in the PRC since the initiative of the Open-door Policy.

Legislation

In a flurry of legislative activity, PRC legislators at both national and regional levels have been producing new regulations, codes and implementing provisions. Foreign investors can encounter difficulties in finding legislation as it is not easily accessible. Even if it is identified, there are even further difficulties in establishing its status and differentiating between the effect of the laws and regulations at national and regional levels. China's legal profession is growing rapidly, but in 1988 there were only 12,335 full-time and 10,359 part-time lawyers and 9,214 public notaries. Traditionally, China prefers to resolve disputes by negotiation in a spirit of mutual understanding and trust; litigation is used only as a last resort. Development of laws as a consequence of the Open-door Policy, however, has resulted in a legal structure that is uncoordinated and complex.

Laws made by the National People's Congress or its standing committee are the highest authority of the PRC, but they frequently resemble statements of general policy, which require detailed implementing regulations. These regulations are usually made by the State Council for national effect and by local government for local effect. Often, the lower the level of government, the more detailed are the provisions. Local implementing regulations are intended to interpret the way in which national provisions will be applied in the local context. In cases of conflict between two sets of laws, the one published by the superior law-making organ will prevail.

Legislation affecting construction falls into two categories — administrative and technical legislation.

Administrative Legislation

Under the category of administrative legislation are laws, regulations and administrative codes. Laws are the highest level of legislation, regulations have a narrower scope than laws, and administrative codes are orders and rules or practical supplements for carrying out laws and regulations. Administrative codes go under a number of names such as notices, detailed principles for practical implementation, methods and administrative rules.

There exists a huge number of administrative codes. All were considered necessary to cope with the practicalities of development taking place in China, but there is now an urgent need to consolidate and develop the legislation relating to construction.

Technical Legislation

Under the category of technical legislation are technical standards, standard rules, standard procedures and standard rates; these are generally referred to as technical codes. Technical codes contribute to standardization of technical matters affecting construction.

Resolving Construction Disputes Involving Foreign Parties

There are four methods of resolving construction disputes, or economic disputes as they are called in the PRC. These are negotiation, mediation, arbitration and litigation.

The first method is friendly negotiation between the parties. This method is popular as it reflects the Chinese philosophy of using mutual trust and friendship in resolving disputes.

The second method, mediation, requires the participation of a third party, who, having no conflict of interest with either party, can therefore be more objective and comprehensive in his or her analysis of the problems than the parties themselves.

Arbitration is the third method of resolving disputes. If a written arbitration agreement exists, then it must be followed. The location of the arbitration is critical. If the arbitration were to take place outside China, normal international practice would apply and Chinese Law would be excluded. Arbitration awards arising from arbitration within China are final and enforceable.

The China International Economic and Trade Arbitration Commission[2] was established in 1989 although its history goes back to 1954 under different names. It appears that the commission deals with all disputes in international business and trade transactions, but it is not clear whether construction disputes are within its scope. A separate commission exists for maritime cases but not for construction.

In 1990, Gulf and Western Marketing was awarded a six figure US Dollar settlement by the Arbitration Court of Shenzhen after a trade dispute with a PRC

---

[2]   Feng Datong, Arbitration gains wider acceptance in dispute resolution. *Standard China Trade*, Sept–Oct 1989, Hong Kong.

company. The settlement gave confidence about future trading with China and showed that the country could honour international trade and legal obligations.

Litigation is the fourth method of resolving disputes. Where there is no arbitration agreement, either party has the right to submit the case to the People's Court for resolution. Such right of litigation is fully safeguarded under Chinese Law.

Negotiation and mediation are by far the most usual and effective means of settling disputes. Arbitration is uncommon and the parties will very rarely resort to litigation.

APPENDIX 1

PROVISIONAL REGULATIONS ON THE GRANTING AND TRANSFERRING OF THE LAND USE RIGHTS OVER THE STATE-OWNED LAND IN CITIES AND TOWNS

Decree of the State Council of the People's Republic of China

No. 55

The Provisional Regulations of the People's Republic of China on the Granting and Transferring of the Land Use Rights over the State-owned Land in Cities and Towns are hereby promulgated and shall take effect on the day of promulgation.

Li Peng

Premier of the People's Republic of China

May 19, 1990

Chapter I   General Provisions

Article 1

These Regulations are formulated for the purpose of reforming the system of using the State-owned land in cities and towns, developing, carrying out rational land utilization and operation, and strengthening the land management and promoting the urban construction and economic development.

Article 2

The State, based on the principle of separation of ownership from land use rights, adopts the system of granting and transferring the land use rights over the State-owned land in cities and towns, excluding the underground resources, buried objects and municipal public utilities.

The State-owned land in cities and towns described in the preceding clause refers to the land under the ownership of the whole people within the scope of cities, county towns, organic towns, industrial and mining areas (hereinafter referred to as the "Land").

Article 3

Unless otherwise specified by the law, all corporations, enterprises, other organizations and individuals, within or outside the territory of the People's Republic of China, may obtain the land use rights and carry out the development, utilization and operation of the Land in accordance with these Regulations.

Article 4

The land use rights obtained by land users in accordance with these Regulations may, within the term of land use, be transferred, leased or mortgaged or exercised in other economic activities. The legitimate rights and interests of the land users shall be protected by the laws of the State.

Article 5

In carrying out the activities of land development, utilization and operation, land users shall comply with the laws and regulations of the State and shall not harm the public interests of the society.

Article 6

The land administration departments of the people's governments above county level shall carry out the supervision and examination of the granting, transferring, leasing, mortgaging and termination of the land use rights in accordance with the law.

Article 7

The registration of the granting, transferring, leasing, mortgaging, and termination of the land use rights and the registration of the buildings or other fixtures shall be handled by the land administration department and housing management department in accordance with the provisions of laws and the relevant regulations of the State Council.

The registration documents are open to public access.

Chapter II   Granting of the Land Use Rights

Article 8

The granting of land use rights refers to the act by which the State, in its capacity as the land owner, grants the land use rights to land users for a certain period of time and the land users pays the State the land granting fees.

The granting of the land use rights shall be effected by a contract.

Article 9

The people's governments of the cities and counties shall be responsible for the granting of the land use rights on a planned and step-by-step basis.

Article 10

The land administration departments of the people's governments of the cities and counties shall, in conjunction with the departments of urban planning and construction management, and departments of housing management, work out programs pertaining to the lots, purposes, duration and other conditions for the granting of the land use rights. Such programs, after approval in accordance with the State Council's regulations on limits of authority, shall be carried out by the land administration departments.

Article 11

The contract for granting the land use rights shall be entered into by and between the land administration departments of the people's governments of cities and counties (hereinafter referred to as the "Grantor") and land users on the principle of equality, free will and compensation.

Article 12

The maximum duration for the granting of the land use rights shall be determined based on the purposes set forth below:

(1) seventy (70) years for residential use;
(2) fifty (50) years for industrial use;
(3) fifty (50) years for educational, scientific and technological, cultural, health and sports uses;
(4) forty (40) years for commercial, tourist and recreational uses; and
(5) fifty (50) years for general or other uses.

Article 13

The land use rights may be granted in any of the following ways:

(1) agreement;
(2) invitation for bids; or
(3) auction.

Detailed procedures and steps for the granting of the land use rights in the ways set out in the preceding clause shall be formulated by the people's governments of provinces, autonomous regions and municipalities under the direct control of the central government.

Article 14

Land users shall, within sixty (60) days after entering into the contract for granting the land use rights, pay the full amount of the land granting fees. In the event that such fees are not paid in full within the time limit, the Grantor shall have the right to rescind the contract and may demand compensation for breach of contract.

Article 15

Grantors shall, in accordance with the contract, grant the land use rights. In the event that the land use rights are not granted in accordance with the contract, the land users shall have the right to rescind the contract and may demand compensation for breach of contract.

Article 16

After paying the land granting fees in full, land users shall, in accordance with the regulations, complete the registration and obtain the land use certificate for the purpose of acquiring the land use rights.

Article 17

Land users shall develop, utilize and operate the Land in accordance with the provisions of the contract for granting the land use rights and the requirements of urban planning.

In case of failure to develop or utilize the land in accordance with the duration and conditions stipulated in the contract, the land administration department of the people's governments of the cities and counties shall correct it and may, according to the seriousness of the case, impose such penalties as warning, fines, or even revocation of the land use rights without compensation.

Article 18

In the event that a land user needs to alter the land use purposes stipulated in its contract for granting land use rights, such land user shall obtain the consent of the Grantors and the the approval of the land administration and municipal planning departments, enter into a separate contract for granting land use rights in accordance with the provisions of this Chapter, adjust the land granting fees and complete the registration.

Chapter III   Transferring of the Land Use Rights

Article 19

The transferring of the land use rights refers to the act by which a land user transfers its land use rights, including sale, exchange and donation.

The land use rights of the Land which has not been developed and utilized by investment in accordance with the duration and conditions stipulated in the contract for granting land use rights shall not be transferred.

Article 20

The transferring of the land use rights shall be effected by a transferring contract.

Article 21

In transferring the land use rights, the rights and obligations set forth in the contract for granting land use rights and registration documents shall be transferred therewith.

Article 22

In the event that a land user obtains its land use rights by way of transferring, the duration of its use shall be the remainder duration after subtracting the period taken by the original land user from that set forth in the contract for granting land use rights.

Article 23

In transferring the land use rights, the ownership of the buildings and other fixtures shall be transferred therewith.

Article 24

The owners or co-owners of the buildings and other fixtures shall enjoy the land use rights over the area occupied by such buildings and fixtures.

In the event that a land user transfers the ownership of the buildings and fixtures, the land use rights over the area occupied by the buildings and fixtures shall be transferred therewith, except under the circumstances where the buildings and fixtures are transferred as movables.

Article 25

In transferring the land use rights and ownership of the buildings and other fixtures, the registration of changed ownership shall be completed in accordance with the regulations.

In the event that the land use rights are transferred separately from the buildings and fixtures, the approval of the land administration and housing management departments above the city or county level shall be obtained and the registration of changed ownership shall be completed in accordance with the regulations.

Article 26

In the event that the prices at which the land use rights are transferred are significantly lower than the market prices, the people's governments of the cities and counties shall have the preemptive right of purchase.

In the event that the market prices at which the land use rights are transferred are unreasonably increased, the people's governments of the cities or counties may take necessary measures.

Article 27

In the event that alteration of land use purpose stipulated in the contract for granting land use rights is necessary, such alteration shall be handled in accordance with Article 18 of these Regulations.

Chapter IV   Leasing of the Land Use Rights

Article 28

The leasing of the land use rights refers to the act by which a land user in its capacity as lessor leases its land use rights together with the buildings and other fixtures to a lessee for use and the lessee pays rent to lessor.

The land use rights on the land which has not been developed and utilized with investment in accordance with the duration and conditions stipulated in the contract for granting land use rights shall not be leased.

Article 29

In the event that the land use rights are leased, the lessor and lessee shall enter into a leasing contract. The leasing contract shall not violate the laws and regulations of the State and the provisions of the contract for granting land use rights.

Article 30

After the land use rights are leased, the lessor must continue to implement the contract for granting land use rights.

Article 31

In the event that the land use rights, buildings and other fixtures are leased, the lessor shall complete the registration in accordance with the regulations.

Chapter V   Mortgaging of the Land Use Rights

Article 32

The land use rights may be mortgaged.

Article 33

In mortgaging the land use rights, the buildings and other fixtures shall be mortgaged therewith. In the event that the buildings and other fixtures are mortgaged, the land use rights over the area occupied by the buildings or fixtures shall be mortgaged therewith.

Article 34

In mortgaging the land use rights, the mortgagor and mortgagee shall enter into a mortgage contract. The mortgage contract shall not violate the laws and regulations of the State and the provisions of the contract for granting land use rights.

Article 35

The mortgage of the land use rights and buildings and other fixtures shall be registered in accordance with the regulations.

Article 36

In the event that a mortgagor fails to pay the debt within the time limit or declares wind-up or bankruptcy during the duration of the mortgage contract, the mortgagee shall have the right to dispose of the mortgaged property in accordance with the laws and regulations of the State and the provisions of the mortgage contract. With respect to the acquisition of the land use rights and ownership of the buildings and other fixtures resulting from the disposal of the mortgaged property, the alteration of changed ownership shall be registered in accordance with the regulations.

Article 37

The mortgage shall enjoy priority in getting paid out of the proceeds from disposal of the mortgaged property.

Article 38

In the event that the mortgage terminates due to the debt repayment or for other reasons, the cancellation of mortgage shall be registered in accordance with the regulations.

Chapter VI   Termination of Land Use Rights

Article 39

The land use rights shall terminate for such reasons as the expiration of the duration set forth in the contract for granting land use rights, the revocation of the land use rights or the extinguishment of the land.

Article 40

Upon the expiration of the land use rights, the State shall obtain the land use rights and the ownership of the buildings and fixtures without compensation. The land users shall return the land use certificates and complete the cancellation of the registration in accordance with the regulations.

Article 41

Upon the expiration of the land use rights, the land users may apply for an extension. If an extension is necessary, the land users shall enter into a new contract, pay the land granting fees and complete the registration in accordance with the provisions set forth in Chapter II of these Regulations.

Article 42

The State shall not revoke ahead of time the land use rights lawfully obtained by land users. Under such special circumstances as may be required for the public interests of the society, the State may, in accordance with the legal procedures, revoke the land use rights ahead of time and shall make appropriate compensation based on the elapsed duration and the actual conditions of the development and utilization of the land in question.

Chapter VII　Allocation of Land Use Rights

Article 43

Allocation of land use rights means that land users obtain by various means the land use rights without compensation in accordance with the laws. Such land users shall pay the land use tax in accordance with the Provisional Regulations of the People's Republic of China on Land Use Tax in Cities and Towns.

Article 44

Allocated land use rights shall not be transferred, leased or mortgaged, except for the circumstances specified in Article 45 of these Regulations.

Article 45

Allocated land use rights with the buildings and fixtures may be transferred, leased or mortgaged, provided that requirements set forth below are met and the approval of the land administration and housing management departments of the people's governments of the cities and counties are obtained:

(1) the land users are corporations, enterprises, other economic organizations or individuals;
(2) the State-owned land use certificates have been obtained;
(3) the legal title certificates of the buildings and fixtures have been obtained; and
(4) contracts for granting land use rights have been entered into in accordance with the provisions of Chapter II of these Regulations; the payment of land granting fees have been made retroactively to the people's governments of the relevant cities or counties or the proceeds from land transferring, leasing or mortgage have been applied against the land use fees. The transferring, leasing and mortgaging of the allocated land use

rights described in the preceding clause shall be conducted in accordance with the provisions of Chapter III, IV and V of these Regulations.

Article 46

With respect to the units or individuals which transfer, lease or mortgage their land use rights without authority, the people's government of the cities and counties shall confiscate their illegitimate proceeds and shall impose penalties according to the seriousness of the offence.

Article 47

In the event that a land user who obtains the allocated land use rights without compensation ceases to use the land due to its relocation, wind-up, termination, bankruptcy or for other reasons, the people's governments of the cities and counties shall revoke the allocated land use rights without compensation and may grant such rights in accordance with the provisions of these Regulations.

The people's governments of the cities or counties may, in order to meet the needs of urban construction, development and planning, revoke the allocated land use rights without compensation and grant such rights in accordance with these Regulations.

In the event that the allocated land use rights are revoked without compensation, the people's governments of the cities or counties shall, according to the specific circumstances, make appropriate compensations for the buildings and other fixtures.

Chapter VIII   Supplementary Provisions

Article 48

The land use rights obtained by individuals in accordance with these Regulations may be inherited.

Article 49

Land users shall pay taxes in accordance with the tax laws and regulations of the State.

Article 50

The land granting fees collected in accordance with these Regulations shall be included in the budget and shall be managed as special funds with the main application to urban construction and land development. Detailed measures on the use and management shall be formulated separately by the Ministry of Finance.

Article 51

The people's governments of provinces, autonomous regions and municipalities under the direct control of the central government shall, in accordance with the provisions of these Regulations and the local conditions, select some cities and towns with appropriate conditions as pilot cities and towns for implementation.

Article 52

With respect to the land developed and operated by foreign investors on a comprehensive basis, the management of the land use rights of such land shall be conducted in accordance with relevant regulations of the State Council.

Article 53

The State Land Administration shall be responsible for the interpretation of these Regulations. The implementing measures shall be formulated by the people's governments of provinces, autonomous regions and municipalities under the direct control of the central government.

Article 54

These Regulations shall come into effect on the day of promulgation.

APPENDIX 2

PROVISIONAL MEASURES FOR THE ADMINISTRATION OF FOREIGN INVESTORS TO DEVELOP AND OPERATE PLOTS OF LAND

Decree of the State Council of the People's Republic of China

No. 56

The Provisional Measures for the Administration of Foreign Investors to Develop and Operate Plots of Land are hereby promulgated and shall take effect on the date of promulgation.

Li Peng

Premier of the People's Republic of China

May 19, 1990

Article 1

These measures are formulated with a view to absorbing foreign investment in the development and operation of plots of land (hereinafter referred to as "plot development"), so as to strengthen the construction of public utilities, improve the investment environment, introduce foreign investment enterprises with advanced technology and exporting products and develop export oriented economy.

Article 2

The plot development described in these measures refers to the activities of carrying out, after obtaining the rights to use state-owned land and pursuant to the plan, comprehensive land development and construction, site level-off and construction of such public utilities as water supply and drainage, electricity and heat supply, road transportation and communication in order to create land use conditions for industry and other constructions and then, transferring the land use rights and operating public utilities or proceeding to construct such surface buildings as industrial and the related production and living facilities as well as the activities of transferring or leasing of such surface buildings.

Specific objectives shall be formulated for any plot development, which shall include construction projects with specific purposes of utilizing the developed land.

Article 3

With respect to any project of plot development for the purpose of absorbing foreign investment, a project proposal for plot development (or a preliminary feasibility study, the same below) shall be formulated under the auspices of the people's government of the city or county.

Any project proposal for plot development which covers less than 1,000 mu[1] of cultivated land or less than 2,000 mu of other types of land and which involves a total amount of investment within the approval authority of the people's government of the province, autonomous region or municipality under the direct control of the central government (including the people's government or the administrative committee of a Special Economic Zone, the same below) shall be submitted for approval to the people's government of the province, autonomous region or municipality under the direct control of the central government.

Any project proposal for plot development which covers more than 1,000 mu of cultivated land or more than 2,000 mu of other types of land and which involves a total amount of investment beyond the approval authority of the people's government of the province, autonomous region or municipality under the direct control of the central government shall be submitted by the people's government of the province, autonomous region and municipality under the direct control of the central government to the State Council for examination and approval after the examination, verification and overall balance thereof by the State Planning Commission.

Article 4

In the event that any foreign investor engages in any plot development, an equity joint

---

[1]   Translator's note: One mu is equal to 1/15 hectare or approximately 0.165 acres.

venture using Chinese and foreign investment, a cooperative joint venture using Chinese and foreign investment or a wholly foreign-owned enterprise shall be established in accordance with the provisions of the Law of the People's Republic of China for Equity Joint Ventures Using Chinese and Foreign Investment, the Law of the People's Republic of China for Cooperative Joint Ventures Using Chinese and Foreign Investment and the Law of the People's Republic of China for Enterprises Using Foreign Investment respectively (hereinafter referred to as "Development Enterprise").

Development Enterprises shall be under the jurisdiction and protection of Chinese laws and all their activities shall be in compliance with the laws and regulations of the People's Republic of China.

Development Enterprises shall have autonomy in their operation and management in accordance with the laws, but shall not have administrative authority within the development areas. The relationship between Development Enterprises and other enterprises is a commercial relationship.

The State encourages the state-owned enterprises to contribute their land use rights to the State-owned land as their investment or conditions for cooperation in order to establish Development Enterprises with foreign investors.

Article 5

Development Enterprises shall, in accordance with the laws, obtain the land use rights to the State-owned land within the development areas.

In the event that the people's government of a city or county in the location of the development areas grants any Development Enterprise the land use rights to the State-owned land, the lots, purposes, duration, land use fees and other conditions [for such land use] shall be rationally determined in accordance with the State laws and administrative regulations on land administration. Contracts for granting the land use rights to the State-owned land shall be entered into and submitted for approval in accordance with the approval authority in granting the land use rights to the State-owned land.

Article 6

After the land use rights to the State-owned land are granted, the ownership of the underground resources and buried objects shall remain with the State. Any development and utilization of such resources shall be administered in accordance with the relevant laws and administrative regulations of the State.

Article 7

Development Enterprises shall draw up the plot development programs or the feasibility study reports which shall clearly stipulate the ultimate and staged objectives of the development and construction, the detailed contents and requirements of the development, and the utilization programs of the developed land.

The plot development programs or the feasibility study reports shall, after being examined and verified by the people's government of the city or county, be submitted for examination and approval to the people's government of the province, autonomous region and municipality under the direct control of the central government. The examination and approval authorities shall organize relevant departments to coordinate the construction and operation of public utilities.

Article 8

Where the development areas are located within the urban planning areas, all development and constructions projects shall meet the requirements of urban planning and shall be subject to the planning control.

All construction projects in the development areas must be undertaken in accordance with the laws, administrative regulations and standards of the State on environmental protection.

Article 9

No land use rights to the State-owned land shall be transferred until Development Enterprises implement the plot development programs, meeting the requirements stipulated in the contracts for granting the land use rights to the State-owned land. Development Enterprises which fail to develop the land with investment in accordance with the conditions stipulated in the contracts for granting the land use rights to the State-owned land and meet the requirements of the plot development programs shall not be allowed to transfer the land use rights to the State-owned land.

Development Enterprises and other enterprises shall transfer, mortgage and terminate the land use rights to the State-owned land in accordance with the laws and administrative regulations of the State on land administration.

Article 10

Development Enterprises may introduce foreign investors to make investment in the development areas, obtain the land use rights to the State-owned land and establish enterprises. Foreign investment enterprises shall be established in accordance with the Law of the People's Republic of China on Equity Joint Ventures Using Chinese and Foreign Investment, the Law of the People's Republic of China on Cooperative Joint Ventures Using Chinese and Foreign Investment and the Law of the People's Republic of China Concerning Enterprises Using Foreign Investment respectively.

The establishment of enterprises in the development areas shall meet the requirements of the industrial policies formulated by the State pertaining to investment. The State encourages the establishment of technologically advanced enterprises and export-oriented enterprises.

Article 11

The post and telecommunication systems in the development areas shall be planned, constructed and operated by the post and telecommunication departments on an overall basis. Alternatively, subject to the approval of the post and telecommunication departments in the province, autonomous region or municipality under the direct control of the central government, the telecommunication systems may be constructed with the investment of Development Enterprises and the post and telecommunication departments, which shall, upon completion, be transferred to the post and telecommunication departments for operation. Such Development Enterprises shall be given economic compensation in accordance with the contract entered into between the parties.

Article 12

The Development Enterprises which make investment in the building of stand-by public utilities for production such as power stations, heat generation stations or water supply stations may engaged in the business of electricity, heat and water supply in the development areas or may transfer such utilities to the local public utility enterprises for operation. Where there is a surplus in the capacity of the public utilities which needs to be supplied out of the [development] areas or to be connected with the inter-area network, the Development enterprises shall enter into contracts with the local public utility enterprises in accordance with the relevant regulations of the State and shall conduct the operation in accordance with the conditions stipulated in the contracts.

The introduction of water and electricity to development areas from outside resources shall be operated by the local public utility enterprises.

Article 13

In the event that the scope of a development area covers any area for construction of coast port or river harbor, the port or harbor area shall be planned and administered by the State on an overall basis. Development Enterprises may, in accordance with the overall plan formulated by the competent transportation departments of the State, construct and operate harbors and docks for special use.

Article 14

No operational and social activities prohibited by laws and administrative regulations of the State shall be allowed within development areas.

Article 15

In the event that special measures are required for the administration of import and export and Customs administration for a development area mainly for the export processing enterprises, such measures shall be submitted to the State Council for approval and the detailed rules shall be formulated by the relevant State departments.

Article 16

The administration, judicial matters, coastal affairs and Customs administration in development areas shall be respectively handled by the competent departments of the State, the local people's government and judicial organs with jurisdiction.

Article 17

Any plot development by corporations, enterprises, other economic organizations or individuals from Hong Kong, Macau and Taiwan shall be carried out with reference to these Measures.

Article 18

These Measures shall come into effect on the date of promulgation in special economic zones, opening coastal cities and open economic zones.

APPENDIX 3

DETAILS OF A SELECTION OF SALES OF LAND USE RIGHTS

Date	City	Area (m^2)	Use	Method of disposal	Purchaser	Price (Rmb¥/m^2)	Term (year)
8.9.1987	Shenzhen	5322	R	negotiation	Shenzhen Industrial Import and Export Corp. of China National Aero-Technology Import and Export Corp.	200	50
15.9.1987	Shenzhen	46355	R	tender	Shenhua Engineering Development Co.	368	50
1.12.1987	Shenzhen	8588	R	auction	Shenzhen SEZ Real Estate Co.	610	50
19.1.1988	Shanghai	3600	C	tender	Hong Kong Pulau Corp.	8515	50
11.2.1988	Fuzhou	3100	C	auction	Hong Kong Yongsheng D. Corp. Ltd.	1484	50
27.4.1988	GETDD	15953	C	auction	n.a.	260	50
25.5.1988	Shenzhen	4691	C	auction	Shenhua Engineering Development Co.	4050	50
25.5.1988*	Shenzhen	9834	R	auction	PRC domestic enterprise	1749	50
2.7.1988	Shanghai	12927	C	auction	Japan Sun Corp. Ltd.	8138	50
7.1988	Xiamen	3195	R/C	auction	Xiamen Industrial and Trade Centre of China	783	70(R) 50(C)

R = Residential, C = Commercial, I = Industrial, D = Dormitory
GETDD = Guangzhou Economic and Technological Development District
n.a. = not available
* The purchaser defaulted in payment of balance of purchase price and the lot was withdrawn.

Date	City	Area (m²)	Use	Method of disposal	Purchaser	Price (Rmb¥/m²)	Term (year)
7.1988	Xiamen	8031	R/C	auction	National Aero-Technology Import and Export Corp. & Xiamen Civil Engineering and Construction Corp.	461	70(R) 50(C)
1.8.1988	Xiamen	3328	R	negotiation	Taiwan Mr Lin	229	50/70
8.8.1988	GETDD	15977	I	tender	n.a.	261	50
30.8.1988	Xiamen	5277	C	negotiation	Singapore Huicheng Corp.	140	50
30.8.1988	Xiamen	91790	R	negotiation	Singapore Huicheng Corp.	124	50/70
30.8.1988	Xiamen	45000	R	negotiation	Singapore Huicheng Corp.	149	50/70
10.9.1988	Xiamen	4648	R	auction	Hong Kong Jian Au China Inc.	1204	50
10.9.1988	Fuzhou	33334	I	negotiation	Hong Kong Yongsheng D. Corp. Ltd.	124	35
10.9.1988	Xiamen	2626	R	auction	Taiwan Mr Wang	850	50
10.9.1988	Xiamen	6000	R	auction	Hong Kong Xinhe Inv. Corp.	804	50
10.9.1988	Xiamen	6030	R	auction	Hong Kong Xinhe Inv. Corp.	790	50
25.9.1988	Shenzhen	7032	C	tender	n.a.	4277	50
5.10.1988	Shenzhen	16455	R	tender	Hong Kong Mr Wang	393	60
28.10.1988	Shenzhen	7291	R	tender	n.a.	2469	50
18.11.1988	Shenzhen	4241	R	auction	n.a.	4716	50
5.12.1988	Xiamen	3820	C	negotiation	American Far-east Bank	207	50
19.12.1988	GETDD	4348	R	negotiation	Sino Group	749	50
19.12.1988	GETDD	8494	I	negotiation	Sino Group	267	50
19.12.1988	GETDD	10145	I	negotiation	Chuang's Group	266	50

Appendix 3

Date	City	Area (m²)	Use	Method of disposal	Purchaser	Price (Rmb¥/m²)	Term (year)
28.12.1988	Shenzhen	12214	R	tender	PRC domestic enterprise	950	50
28.12.1988	Shenzhen	3564	C	tender	PRC domestic enterprise	2273	50
6.1.1989	GETDD	8419	I	tender	Wall Hill Development	275	50
6.1.1989	GETDD	4333	R/C	tender	Power Sky Development	725	50
16.1.1989	GETDD	4054	R/C	tender	Chinney Construction	822	50
21.1.1989	GETDD	4105	R/C	tender	Ka Wah Stones	812	50
21.1.1989	Shanghai	3600	R/C	tender	Hong Kong Potto Investment Company Ltd.	14720	50
25.2.1989	Xiamen	3155	R	auction	Sino Group	2440	n.a.
25.2.1989	Xiamen	3326	R	auction	Sino Group	2375	n.a.
25.2.1989	Xiamen	4125	R	auction	Sino Group	2424	n.a.
25.2.1989	Xiamen	1182	R/C	auction	Tokyo Transport and Warehouse Co.	3469	n.a.
28.2.1989	GETDD	10903	I	tender	Lee Kum Kee Group	263	50
1.4.1989	Shenzhen	9571	R	tender	PRC domestic enterprise	1536	50
29.4.1989	GETDD	10184	I	tender	Star Light Group	280	50
2.5.1989	GETDD	4936	R/C	tender	Sino Group	1005	50
13.5.1989	Shenzhen	11500	I	tender	PRC domestic enterprise	842	30
6.6.1989	Shenzhen	5207	R	tender	PRC domestic enterprise	1360	50
20.6.1989	Shenzhen	10000	I	tender	PRC domestic enterprise	620	30

R = Residential, C = Commercial, I = Industrial, D = Dormitory
GETDD = Guangzhou Economic and Technological Development District
n.a. = not available

Date	City	Area (m²)	Use	Method of disposal	Purchaser	Price (Rmb¥/m²)	Term (year)
11.10.1989	Shenzhen	6072	I	negotiation	PRC domestic enterprise	125	n.a.
22.11.1989	Shenzhen	28063	I	negotiation	PRC domestic enterprise	166	n.a.
4.1990	Shenzhen	22585	R	tender	PRC domestic enterprise	1501	50
5.1990	Shenzhen	13576	D	tender	PRC domestic enterprise	604	50
16.5.1990	Shenzhen	30069	R	tender	PRC domestic enterprise	1596	50
16.5.1990	Shenzhen	30544	R	tender	PRC domestic enterprise	1571	50
16.5.1990	Shenzhen	21257	R	tender	PRC domestic enterprise	1647	50

APPENDIX 4

TENDER DOCUMENTS FOR A SITE IN GUANGZHOU ECONOMIC AND TECHNOLOGICAL DEVELOPMENT DISTRICT

(Unofficial translation for reference only)

SUMMARY OF PARTICULARS AND

CONDITIONS OF SALE BY

TENDER

Lot No. GQ-B7-2

GUANGZHOU ECONOMIC & TECHNOLOGICAL

DEVELOPMENT DISTRICT

VACANT POSSESSION OFFERED FOR SALE

BY

TENDER

TENDER CLOSES AT 12:00 NOON ON 27TH APRIL, 1989

(THURSDAY)

Particulars of the Property

1. The Property:

    Lot No. GQ-B7-2 in Guangzhou Economic & Technological Development District, Guangzhou, People's Republic of China.

2. Land Use Right Period:

    50 years.

3. Annual Land Use Tax:

    The annual land use tax shall be in accordance with the National Regulation. The present fee is Rmb¥2.0 per square metre each year as stipulated by the Administrative Committee of Guangzhou Economic & Technological Development District.

4. Registered Site Area:

    10,184 square metres or thereabouts

5. Development Conditions:

    (1) Permitted Us: Industrial
    (2) Site Coverage: 45%
    (3) Plot Ratio: 3.6
    (4) Total permitted building floor area: not exceeding 36,662 square metres thereabouts.
    (5) Building Height: 8 storeys above ground.
         Total building height cannot exceed 40 metres above ground.
    (6) Set back conditions:
         East: 10 metres; West: 10 metres; North: 15 metres; South: not less than half of the height of the building and 5 metres.
    (7) The overall building scheme shall be in harmony with the surrounding environment.
    (8) Finishing requirements: Internal and External Finishing are subject to the building design approval.
    (9) Parking area: Not less than 1,200 square metres.
    (10) The general site formation level is 0.3 metre higher than the average level of the four corners.
    (11) Greenery: Not less than 20% of site area.
    (12) Ingress and Egress: In north side.
    (13) All building design shall adhere to existing Building Design Standards and Regulations of Peoples' Republic of China.

6. Design and Construction

    (1) The Grantee shall within 12 months from signing of the Grant Contract submit to the Construction Bureau design drawings, working and construction program. The Construction Bureau shall give comment or approval within 60 days upon receiving such drawings. If no response is received after 60 days, it shall be treated that approval has been granted.
    (2) The Grantee should commence the construction in accordance with the approved planning and construction drawing within 14 months upon the signing of Grant Contract.

(3)   The Grantee shall complete all construction work within 4 years from the date
      of obtaining the 'Land Use Certificate'. Extension of the completion date may
      be granted but shall not exceed one year subject to a fine of 10% of the grant
      premium.

7. Closing Date of Tender:

12:00 noon on 27th April, 1989 (Thursday).

This English version is for reference only. Please refer to the Chinese version of this
Tender Document. Whilst care has been taken in preparing these Particulars of the
property no warranty or representation is given or implied as to the accuracy of any of
the content, nor any plans hereto annexed (if any).

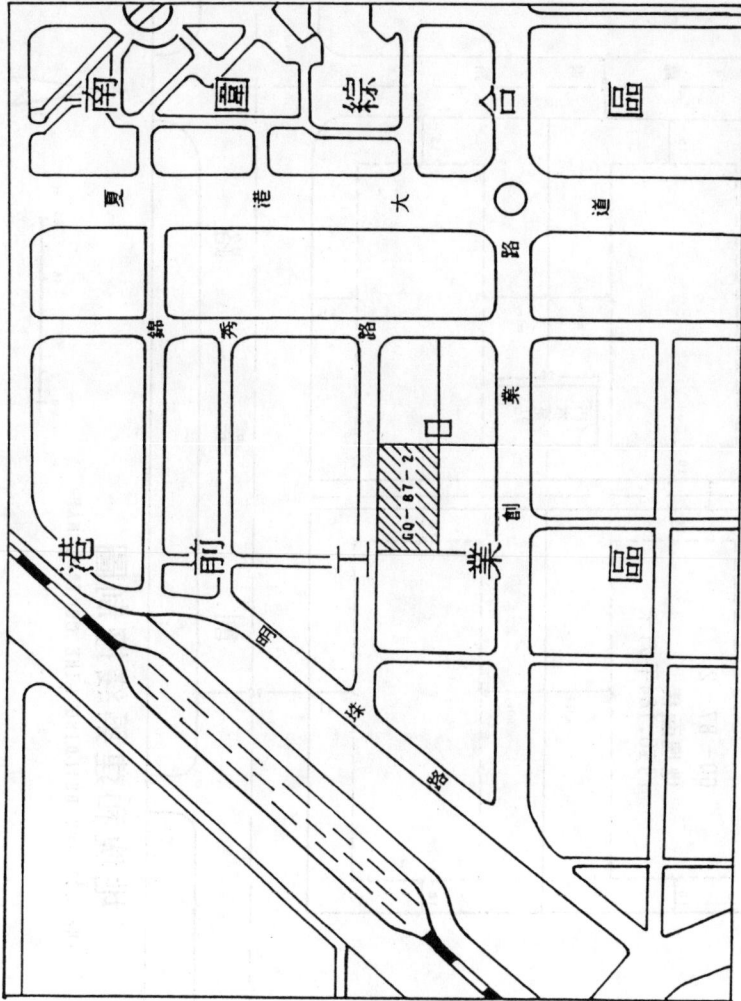

地塊位置圖

LOT LOCATION

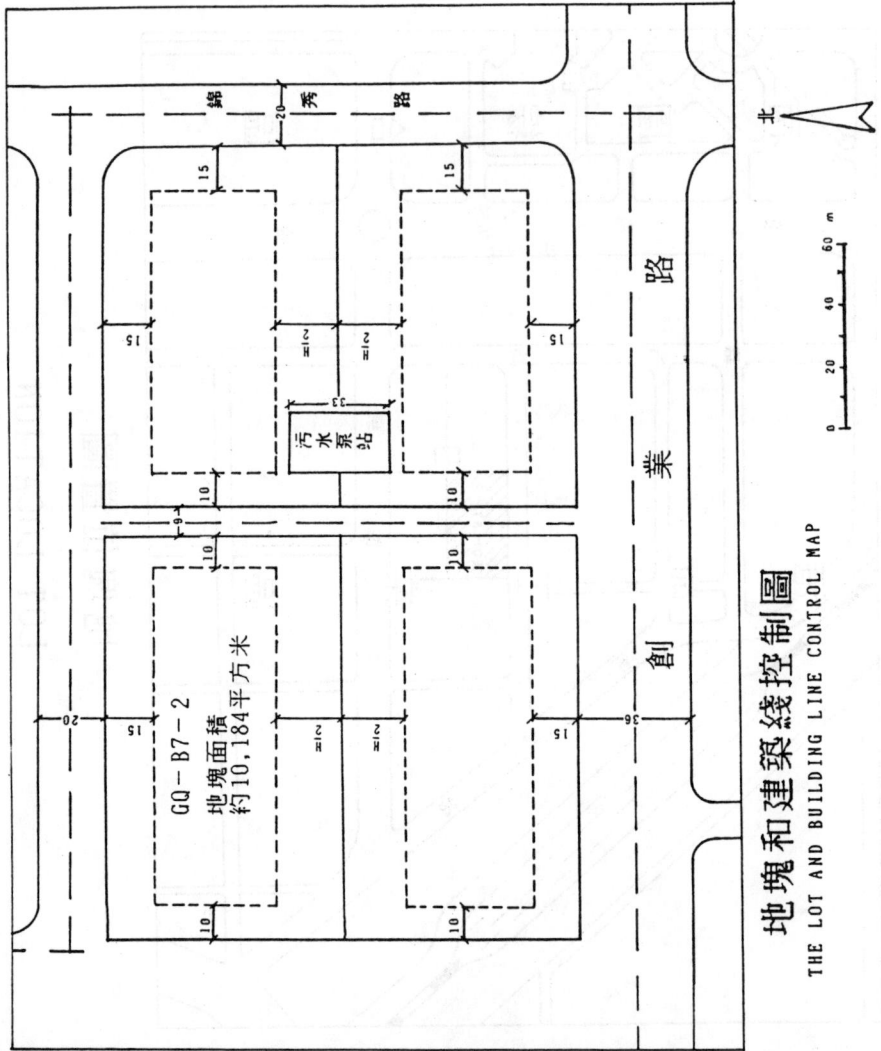

地塊和建築綫控制圖

THE LOT AND BUILDING LINE CONTROL MAP

APPENDIX 5

DEVELOPMENT CONDITIONS FOR A LOT IN SHANGHAI HONGQIAO ECONOMIC AND TECHNOLOGICAL DEVELOPMENT ZONE

(Unofficial translation for reference only)

THE GRANT OF LAND USE RIGHTS FOR
VALUABLE CONSIDERATION OF LOT
NO. 26 IN SHANGHAI HONGQIAO
ECONOMIC AND TECHNOLOGICAL
DEVELOPMENT ZONE

TENDER DOCUMENTS

TENDER NOTICE

GRANT AND USE CONDITIONS

TENDER FORM

ACCEPTANCE NOTICE

GRANT CONTRACT OF LAND USE RIGHTS

The Shanghai Land Administration Bureau

March 22, 1988

3. Development Conditions:

3.1 Permitted Use:

Lot No. 26 -	office or hotel or office and hotel combined; or build according to the use stipulated in Lot No. 26A and Lot No.26B;
Lot No.26A -	apartments or office or hotel; or apartments, office and/or hotel combined;
Lot No.26B -	apartments or office or hotel; or apartments, office and/or hotel combined;

3.2 Site Coverage:

Lot No.26 -	not exceeding 55% (for office or hotel, or office and hotel combined only);
Lot No.26A -	apartments not exceeding 45% office, hotel and/or apartments combined not exceeding 55%;
Lot No.26B -	apartments not exceeding 45%; office, hotel and/or apartments combined not exceeding 55%

3.3 Plot Ratio:

Lot No.26 -	not exceeding 60,000 sq. metres/hectare (for office or hotel, or office and hotel combined only);
Lot No.26A -	apartments not exceeding 42,000 sq. metres/hectare; office or hotel, or apartments, office and/or hotel combined not exceeding 50,000 sq. metres/hectare;
Lot No.26B -	apartments not exceeding 42,000 sq. metres/hectare; office or hotel, or apartments, office and/or hotel combined not exceeding 50,000 sq. metres/hectare.

3.4 Height Limit (from ground level): 120 metres.

3.5 Greenery: Not less than 20% of the site area.

3.6 Vehicular Ingress and Egress at the following positions:

Lot No.26 -	west, north;
Lot No.26A -	north;
Lot No.26B -	west, north.

3.7 Car Parking Requirement:

(a) Hotel not less than 0.3 private-car parking space per guest room;
(b) Apartments not less than 1 private-car parking space per apartment;
(c) Offices not less than 0.5 private-car parking space per 100 square metres of building area;
(d) Requirements for the parking of large motor vehicles and bicycles and for the parking, loading and unloading of service vehicles and the turnaround of all vehicles should also be provided.

• High-rise buildings shall provide for civil defence purposes a basement of the same size and situation as far as possible with the surrounding buildings, boundary walls, squares, greenery, roads and the environment in general.
• The overall layout of the development and the design of individual buildings shall be in harmony as far as possible with the surrounding buildings, boundary walls, squares, greenery, roads and the environment in general.

- South-facing windows of residences situated on the lowest floors in the northern side of individual buildings, in particular high-rise buildings shall receive between the hours of 9:00 and 15:00 Beijing time on the day of Winter Solstice full-window day-lighting of not less than one hour.

  Building design drawings shall be accompanied by diagrams showing natural lighting which shall be based on a latitude of 30°21' N for the Shanghai area and an angle of the sun at noon on the day of Winter Solstice of 35°21' N.

- The outdoor site formation level shall be higher than the level at the centre of major roads in the vicinity by not less than 0.3 metre.

- The Grantee shall strictly adhere to the Lot and Building Line Control Map in the design of the overall and individual buildings, including the basements therein. The Lot and Building Line Control Map is attached.

- The definitions of site coverage and plot ratio in the Conditions are respectively:

  (a) Site Coverage: the ratio (expressed as a percentage) of the total area of the Lot covered by a building or buildings and the area of the Lot itself;

  (b) Plot Ratio: the ratio of the total building floor area within the Lot and the area of the Lot, expressed in 0,000 sq. metre/hectare.

APPENDIX 6

REGULATIONS FOR THE TRANSFER OF LAND USE RIGHTS FOR VALUABLE CONSIDERATION IN SHANGHAI CITY (1987)

(Promulgated by the Shanghai Municipal People's Government on 29th November, 1987 — Unofficial translation for reference only)

Part I   General

Section 1

To promote comprehensive reform and the open policy, to reform the land use system, to implement the Transfer of Land Use Rights for Valuable Consideration, and to foster economic developments of Shanghai, these Regulations are enacted in accordance with relevant provisions of the State.

Section 2

In these Regulations:

(1)   "Transfer of Land Use Rights for Valuable Consideration" means economic activities related to the development of land and buildings through the grant and assignment of land use rights for valuable consideration.

(2)   "Grant of Land Use Rights for Valuable Consideration" (hereinafter referred to as"Grant") means the provision by the Shanghai Municipal People's Government (hereinafter referred to as "Government") of specific lots of land owned by the State, under stipulated term of years, use and any other conditions for a grantee or grantees to explore and develop, in consideration of the payment of premium and ground rent.

(3)   "Assignment of Land Use Rights" (hereinafter referred to as "Assignment") means the passing of land use rights by a grantee or grantees after such land use rights have been granted.

(4)   "The Premium for Land Use Rights" (hereinafter referred to as "Premium") means the monetary consideration payable to the Government in return for the grant of land use rights.

(5)   "Ground Rent" means the annual monetary consideration payable by a grantee or grantees to the Government in return for the continuous right to the use of the land.

(6)   "Grantee" means an enterprise, other economic organization, or person that obtains land use rights by way of Grant, and shall where the context permits, include his assignees and other successors in title.

Section 3

Ownership of land by the People's Republic of China is not affected by the Transfer of Land Use Rights for Valuable Consideration.

Underground natural resources, minerals, and objects buried or hidden in the land shall not form part of the Transfer of Land Use Rights for Valuable Consideration.

Section 4

No enterprise, economic organization, or person shall be a Grantee unless such enterprise, economic organization, or person are registered in or are of nationalities of states or territories with which the People's Republic of China maintains diplomatic relationship or with which trade delegation or delegations is maintained.

Section 5

The lawful rights of Grantees are protected by law.

All activities arising out of the Transfer of Land use Rights for Valuable Consideration shall comply with the relevant laws and regulations of the People's Republic of China and with regulations of Shanghai.

Section 6

The Shanghai Land Administration Bureau (hereinafter referred to as the "Land Bureau") shall be responsible for matters relating to the Transfer of Land Use Rights for Valuable Consideration in Shanghai. The Grant Contract of Land Use Rights (hereinafter referred to as the "Grant Contract") shall be signed between the Land Bureau and the Grantee.

Section 7

The Shanghai Land and Building Registration Office (hereinafter referred to as the "Registration Office") shall be responsible for matters relating to registration of the Transfer of Land Use Rights for Valuable Consideration. Documents registered shall be made available for public inspection.

Section 8

The maximum term of any Grant shall be determined by the Land Bureau subject to the following limits:

(1)	land for entertainment use	20 years
(2)	land for industrial use	40 years
(3)	land for private residential use	50 years
(4)	land for hotel, commercial, office use	50 years
(5)	land for scientific, technological, cultural and medical use	50 years
(6)	land for composite or other use	50 years

Terms exceeding the above limits shall require approval by the Government on application by the Land Bureau.

Section 9

Unless otherwise stated in the Grant Contract, or disallowed for town planning reasons, the term may be extended on application by the Grantee. The maximum period of extension shall be determined by the Land Bureau in accordance with Section 8 of these Regulations. Extension of the term shall be granted under a new Grant Contract and in consideration of a Premium.

Section 10

Unless otherwise stated in the Grant Contract, any Grantee may assign, mortgage, charge, or generally pledge land use rights as security.

Such assignments, mortgages, charges, or pledges shall be invalid unless made in accordance with these Regulations.

Section 11

Grantees that are foreign enterprises engaged in investment shall have the privilege under certain regulations of not paying Ground Rent as provided for in "Procedures of Shanghai Municipality for the Administration of the Use of Land in Chinese–Foreign Joint Ventures". Grantees that obtain land use rights other than by means of these Regulations shall pay land use fees under "Procedures of Shanghai Municipality for the Administration of the Use of Land in Chinese–Foreign Joint Ventures".

Section 12

Operators of economic activities on any land the right to use of which is obtained under these Regulations shall, according to provisions, apply to relevant authorities for approval, and conduct business registration and tax registration.

Part II   Grant of Land Use Rights for Valuable Consideration

Section 13

Lots that form the subject of Grant shall be identified and the conditions of Grant shall be prepared by the Bureau of Shanghai City Planning and Building Construction Administration (hereinafter referred to as the "Planning and Building Bureau") and the Shanghai Municipal Housing Administration Bureau (hereinafter referred to as the "Housing Bureau"). Implementation shall proceed after approval by the Government.

Section 14

Grants of land use rights may be made by the Land Bureau by means of direct grant or tender by invitation, etc.

Section 15

The Land Bureau shall supply all prospective Grantees with the following information and provisions:

(1)   the location, bearing, measurement area and topographical plan of the lot;
(2)   the planned use, building covenant period, minimum building cost to be expended and the minimum floor area to be developed;
(3)   plot ratio, site coverage, height limit and such other planning requirements;
(4)   environmental protection, greenery, sanitary and hygiene provisions, traffic and fire prevention and fighting requirements;
(5)   the existing state of public utilities and planned construction or construction requirements;
(6)   surface conditions of the subject lot;
(7)   form of Grant and the term;
(8)   qualifications of tenderers;
(9)   location for depositing tenders, tender closing date and tender procedures, requirements, conditions and criteria for selecting tenders;
(10)   the amount of initial deposit to be paid at the time of tendering;
(11)   payment terms and requirement of the Premium and the financial obligations of the Grantee;
(12)   specific conditions and methods regarding Grant and Assignment;
(13)   form of the Grant Contract;
(14)   requirements regarding the sale and management of buildings;
(15)   others.

Section 16

Procedure of direct Grant:

(1)   Necessary details of the lot to be granted and the conditions of the proposed Grant are provided by the Land Bureau to the intending Grantee of the land use rights.
(2)   The intending grantee having obtained such information as in (1) above, shall within the prescribed time limit submit to the Land Bureau, a scheme of the proposed development, the Premium proposal and the payment terms.
(3)   On receipt of the documents submitted under (2) above, the Land Bureau shall communicate its decision to the intending Grantee within 30 days.
(4)   The Grant Contract shall be signed between the Land Bureau and the Grantee on payment by the Grantee of a second deposit, the amount of Premium having been agreed upon by both parties through consultation.
(5)   The grantee shall pay the Premium as prescribed in the Grant Contract, obtain from the Land Bureau a Land Use Rights Certificate and register the land use rights with the Registration Office within the prescribed time.

Section 17

Procedure of Tender by Invitation:

(1)   The Land Bureau shall issue invitations to tender, tender documents and specific information regarding the tender to parties so invited, having taken into account the requirements of the subject lot.
(2)   Tenderers shall before the prescribed time, deposit duly sealed tenders into a

specified tender box, and pay to the body specified the initial deposit which shall not bear any interest.

(3)   A Tender Assessment Panel shall be formed and shall be constituted of the Land Bureau, appropriate Government departments and experts, and shall be responsible for opening, assessing and selecting tenders.

The Tender Assessment Panel may invalidate tenders that are submitted by unqualified tenderers, or that are not in accordance with the conditions of the tender documents or that are submitted out of the prescribed time.

The Land Bureau shall issue to the successful tenderer at the address shown in the Tender Form an Acceptance Notice after a Selection Notice has been issued by the Tender Assessment Panel. Tenders shall be opened, assessed and selected before the Shanghai Notary Public Office, which shall issue certification to this effect.

(4)   The Grant Contract shall be signed before the prescribed time with the Land Bureau and the second deposit paid by the successful tenderer who shall present at the same time the Acceptance Notice.

(5)   The successful tenderer shall pay according to the Grant Contract the Premium, obtain from the Land Bureau a Land Use Rights Certificate and register the land use rights with the Registration Office within the prescribed time.

Section 18

The right to a Grant shall be cancelled if the successful tenderer does not sign the Grant Contract with the Land Bureau within the prescribed time and the initial deposit shall be forfeited. However an extension may be applied for to the Land Bureau within 10 days before the expiration of the prescribed time and any extension so permitted shall not exceed 30 days.

The initial deposit submitted by the successful tenderer may be applied towards the Premium. Initial deposits submitted by unsuccessful tenderers shall be returned within the prescribed time at the tenderers' address.

Section 19

The second deposit may also be applied towards the Premium. Grantees shall not be entitled to a refund of such deposit if obligations under the Grant Contract are not fulfilled. The Land Bureau shall repay an amount equivalent to two times the second deposit if obligations on its part are not fulfilled.

Section 20

The Grant Contract signed between the Land Bureau and the Grantee shall be notarized by the Shanghai Notary Public Office.

Section 21

The Premium shall be paid in the currency specified in the Grant Contract.

Section 22

Ground Rent the amount of which as prescribed below shall be payable for each year by the Grantee:

(1)   Rmb¥1,000 in respect of any lot having an area of 1,000 square metres or below;
(2)   Rmb¥1 per square metre for any lot having an area in excess of 1,000 square metres.

Section 23

Any proposal to modify any condition of the Grant Contract in respect of the nature of land use and planning requirements shall be submitted to the Land Bureau. The Land Bureau shall refer any such application to the Planning and Building Bureau for approval. Consent to modify shall only be given after payment by the Grantee of a modification premium, whereupon a new Grant Contract or a Supplementary Contract shall be signed and registered.

Section 24

Any proposal to erect buildings or install services on land granted shall be submitted for prior approval in accordance with the planning, construction management, building management, traffic, environmental protection, hygiene, sanitation, fire prevention and fighting and such other provisions for the purposes of municipal administration.

Section 25

A fine may be levied by the Land Bureau according to circumstances and ultimately the land may be re-entered into by the Land Bureau if the Grantee fails to complete the development as specified in the Grant Contract.

Part III   The Assignment of Land Use Rights

Section 26

Land use rights shall not be assigned before completion of the development as specified in the Grant Contract. Assignment of the right to use only part of the land originally granted shall require the prior approval of the Land Bureau.

Section 27

Assignment of land use rights shall also mean gift, sale, or exchange of the same.

Section 28

The right to use the part of the land occupied by the building (including courtyards, gardens and boundary walls) shall be assigned at the same time as such building is assigned by the Grantee. In the event of a building being sub-divided and so assigned, the owners of parts of the building shall own corresponding portions of the land use rights, and the land use rights of the whole building shall remain in unity.

Prior to sale of a building by sub-division, the vendor shall specify the shares of land use rights allocated to the purchasers of the various parts and draw up a Deed of Mutual Covenant in accordance with the requirements of the Housing Bureau.

Sale of buildings prior to completion of construction shall require the prior approval of the Housing Bureau.

Section 29

The Grant Contract together with all rights, liabilities and obligations duly registered in the register shall run with the Assignment or succession of land use rights.

Section 30

The Assignment may be conducted within or outside the territory of China, except in countries or territories with which the People's Republic of China has no diplomatic relationship or with which no trade delegation or delegations are maintained.

Assignments conducted outside China shall be notarized locally, and duly confirmed by the foreign affairs department and the consulate or trade delegation of the People's Republic of China. Assignments conducted within China shall be notarized by the Shanghai Notary Public Office or any other duly authorized organ.

The succession of land use rights except as a result of the mediation or judgement of the law courts shall be notarized by the Shanghai Notary Public Office.

Section 31

Any Assignment shall be invalid unless the assignee of land use rights and buildings in accordance with Section 30 of these Regulations carries out transfer procedures by producing to the Land Bureau and the Housing Bureau notarized or confirmed Assignment Contracts or probate documents. A transfer fee and tax shall be payable.

Section 32

The Assignment and succession of land use rights (including any building etc.), having been duly signed by the assignee on the Assignment contract or notarized in the case of succession, shall be registered in the Registration Office.

Section 33

Any proposal to modify any condition of the Grant Contract in respect of the land use and planning requirements shall be treated in accordance with Section 23 of these Regulations.

Section 34

Land use rights are deemed to be assigned when the ownership of any enterprise or economic organization is transferred, and such deemed assignment shall be treated as Assignment and in accordance with these Regulations.

Part IV   Mortgage

Section 35

The right to use land and building and other improvements on the land may be mortgaged. Mortgages shall be registered at the Registration Office.

Section 36

The rights and obligations of mortgagees and mortgagors shall be stated in the Mortgage Deed which shall not contravene any provision in the Grant Contract.

Section 37

The tenancy relationship in respect of part or the whole of a building or buildings shall not be affected by a mortgage or mortgages of the same.

Section 38

Mortgagees have a preferred right to repayment. The order of repayment among mortgagees of the same building or part of a building shall be in accordance with the order of registration.

Section 39

Mortgagees may, acting in accordance with provisions of the laws and the Mortgage Deed, dispose of mortgaged property in the event that the mortgagor does not repay the mortgage loan as provided, or enters into liquidation or becomes bankrupt during the mortgage term.

Assignees who obtain Assignment together with any building or buildings and other improvements on the land by way of mortgage action shall obtain notarization and confirmation in accordance with Section 30 of these Regulations and shall proceed with transfer and registration procedures in accordance with Section 31 and Section 32 of these Regulations.

Section 40

Mortgagors and mortgagees shall register cancellation of mortgages at the Registration Office as and when mortgages are cancelled as a result of repayment of loan or for other reasons.

Part IV   Re-Possession of Land Use Rights

Section 41

On expiration of the term of years as contained in the Grant Contract, the land use rights in respect of the land shall be re-possessed by the Land Bureau. The Land Bureau shall simultaneously cancel the Land Use Rights Certificate and notify the Registration Office for the lot to be de-registered. Building or buildings on the lot together with any other improvement shall pass on to the Land Bureau without compensation.

The Grantee shall demolish and remove technological equipments as required by the Grant Contract. unless otherwise stated in the Grant Contract, building or buildings not designed and constructed for general use shall be demolished and removed at the expense of the Grantee.

Section 42

Land use rights before the expiration of the term granted shall not be re-possessed. Under special circumstances the Land Bureau acting in the interest of the public and in accordance with lawful procedure may re-possess in consideration of reasonable compensation.

The Land Bureau shall, six months before the re-possession of any land use rights, serve a notice on the Grantee giving reasons of the re-possession, the bearing and the boundary of the lot, and the date of re-possession. Such notice shall also be affixed on the lot concerned. The land use rights together with building or buildings and any other improvement shall pass onto the Land Bureau as from the date stated in the notice.

Section 43

The amount of compensation for re-possession before expiration of the term granted shall be subject to consultation between the Land Bureau and the Grantee, account to be taken of the remaining term, the nature of land use, the values of the building and buildings and any other improvements on the land, and the Premium paid for the Grant. In case of dispute, either party may instigate legal proceedings. The re-possession date specified in the notice shall not be affected by any proceeding that may have been instigated.

Section 44

Subject to consultation with the Grantee and in exchange for the unexpired land use right of a lot, the Land Bureau may offer to the Grantee the land use right of another lot. The monetary consideration of such an exchange shall be based on the difference in value between the original lot and the new lot. A new Grant Contract shall be signed between the Land Bureau and the Grantee in respect of the new lot so exchanged. The Grantee shall thereafter proceed with the procedures of registration and exchange of Land Use Rights Certificate.

Part VI   Taxation

Section 45

Following the signing of the Grant Contract or Assignment, the Grantee shall register for tax purposes with the Shanghai Tax Office (hereinafter referred to as the "Tax Office") and pay contract tax in accordance with Rules for the Implementation of Shanghai Municipal Provisional Regulations on Contract Tax. The rate of contract tax shall be half of the rate specified therein. Contract tax in respect of any Grant by the Government is hereby exempted.

Section 46

The following rates of contract tax shall apply in cases of Assignment together with building or buildings, the purchase price or the prevailing market value of which shall be reported by the assignee and subject to confirmation by Shanghai Municipal Taxation Bureau:

Sale — 3% of transaction price
Gift — 3% of prevailing market value
Exchange — 3% of prevailing market value

Section 47

The Grantee shall pay, in respect of building or buildings erected on the lot granted and in accordance with the Provisional Regulations Governing City House Property Tax, real estate tax which shall be at the annual rate of 1.2 per cent of the original value of the building or buildings less 20%, and shall be payable by two instalments.

Newly-constructed buildings in the Economic and Technological Development Zone shall be exempt from real estate tax for five years beginning from the date when the construction has been accomplished.

Section 48

The Grantee shall pay, in the event of assignment or lease of the building or buildings with the land use rights, in accordance with the Regulations of the People's Republic of China on Consolidated Industrial and Commercial Tax, Consolidated Industrial and Commercial Tax after the completion of the buildings at the following rates:

3% of the income from selling in the case of sale;
5% of the income from the rent in the case of rent.

Besides, a Grantee shall pay income tax for his own business proceeds in accordance with the relevant tax laws. In the case of sale or rent by individuals the income tax shall be paid pursuant to the Individual Income Tax Law of the People's Republic of China.

Part VII   Supplementary Provisions

Section 49

Tax payable by Grantees who are business enterprises or economic organizations of the People's Republic of China shall in the first instance be in accordance with provisions applicable to such enterprises or economic organizations. These Regulations shall apply to foreign enterprises.

Section 50

Economic disputes arising out of the Transfer of Land Use Rights for Valuable Consideration may be referred to a Chinese arbitrator or other arbitrators in accordance with the arbitration clause in the Grant Contract or any other written arbitration agreement entered into by parties concerned.

Parties to a dispute may, in the absence of any arbitration clause in the contract or of any arbitration agreement subsequent to the dispute, refer the matter to the law courts in accordance with the laws of the People's Republic of China.

Section 51

These Regulations shall be interpreted by the Legal Affairs Office of Shanghai Municipal Government.

Section 52

Implementation of these Regulations shall be determined by the Land Bureau and other Government departments and shall be carried out on approval by the Government.

Section 53

Any amendment to these Regulations shall not have retroactive effect on contracts signed prior to such amendment. Any amendment that confers privileges onto a Grantee provided they are not disallowed by laws of the State may take retroactive effect on application by the Grantee.

Section 54

These Regulations shall take effect on 1st January, 1988.

INDEX